RECLAIMING

✷

MORALITY

IN

AMERICA

RECLAIMING
✳
MORALITY
IN
AMERICA

William Murchison

THOMAS NELSON PUBLISHERS
Nashville • Atlanta • London • Vancouver

Published in Nashville, Tennessee, by Thomas Nelson, Inc., Publishers, and distributed in Canada by Word Communications, Ltd., Richmond, British Columbia, and in the United Kingdom by Word (UK), Ltd., Milton Keynes, England.

Scripture quotations are from The Holy Bible, KING JAMES VERSION.

Library of Congress Cataloging-in-Publication Data

Murchison, William P.
  Reclaiming morality in America / William Murchison.
    p. cm.
  Includes bibliographical references.
  ISBN 0–7852–8168–1
1. United States—Moral conditions. I. Title.
HN90.M6M87 1994   94–11492
306'.0973—dc20   CIP

Printed in the United States of America

1 2 3 4 5 6 7 - 00 99 98 97 96 95 94

For Nancy

CONTENTS

FOREWORD

by William Bennett

William Murchison, a political commentator with a philosophical bent, has written an eloquent and important book about America's moral crisis. *Reclaiming Morality in America* addresses our nation's moral decline, its consequences, and the prospects for recovery. And recovery is what we desperately need.

During the last three decades, American society has experienced substantial social regression. In recent years, and across the political spectrum, a consensus has emerged that something has gone wrong at the core. As Murchison writes, "a moral transformation of vast proportions has occurred in our midst. The standards to which we adhere in every area are not higher than before; they are dramatically lower." And so they are.

A decade or so ago, individuals who believed in time-honored moral codes and who argued that there are absolute standards of right and wrong were dismissed as "moralizers."

That was then.

Today we are seeing the terrible human cost—the rising body count—of America's moral transformation. It is being played out every day on our urban streets, in hospital emergency rooms, in our courts, in congregate care facilities, and in our classrooms.

This is now.

It is not surprising, then, that people are searching for ways to become a more civilized society. To which one might respond: this book is a good place to start. There are several things which distinguish this book from many others which address the "values" issue, as Murchison refers to it.

First is its calm and civilized tone. This is an impressive achievement when you consider that *Reclaiming Morality in*

America deals with some of the most contentious issues in contemporary political life: abortion, euthanasia, pornography, homosexuality, family life, education, crime and punishment, and religion and faith, to name a few.

Second, *Reclaiming Morality in America* relies on rigorous thought and sound empirical analysis. Many commentators resort to unsupported assertions and political slogans when trying to present their case. Bill Murchison tells you not only what he believes, he tells you why he believes certain things. He is a practitioner of the best kind of political debate—the kind of debate which relies on facts, persuasion, argument. Even those who disagree with his conclusions should concede that Murchison provides a strong intellectual defense of them.

Third, Bill Murchison resists the temptation to simply blame others for the degraded state of our culture—"a culture we have made with our own hands and hearts," he points out. Murchison doesn't simply rationalize away one of the hard truths of modern times; Americans have gotten used to decadence. He recognizes our condition, and he urges us—he implores us—to do better and to be better, because decadence is not a good thing to get used to.

What, then, do we do? Murchison devotes the second half of his book to providing specific answers to that question. But if there is a single, central prescription that Bill Murchison believes will turn things around, it is the need for Americans to affirm again the spiritual view of life that undergirds the moral vision. It is refreshing to see someone strong and sure in his faith. Here is a man unafraid to make the link between morality and culture on the one hand, and religion and God guiding that hand.

"The world is forwarded by having its attention fixed on the best things," Matthew Arnold once wrote. *Reclaiming Morality in America* fixes our attention on the best things. It provides a compelling case for the need for virtue, for character, for moral verities. It reminds us of the high stakes involved, and if we prevail, the better world that awaits us.

ACKNOWLEDGMENTS

Nothing in this book is strictly original. The author says so with considerable pride and satisfaction. The last thing the world needs is another "original" view of morality and moral responsibility. We have had a succession of those in our tumultuous time. They are at the heart of our problem, in fact. Fresh angles of vision have produced fresh outrages of the Vision itself, to the point that twentieth-century morality is, more than anything else, a do-it-yourself enterprise.

Numerous friends, colleagues, and family members have nonetheless communicated valuable insights to me—without the slightest notion they were doing anything of the kind. They are too many to single out. I hope they will accept my gratitude anyway.

Not in the least or lightest debt payable is to the editors and varied personnel of Thomas Nelson, who have treated me with civility, tact, and courtesy. These are attributes one is glad to see have not vanished altogether from the business world in our flustered times. Bruce Nygren, my editor, has rendered judgments calculated, as I saw instantly, to make a raw manuscript not only more accessible but more credible. I am grateful to Sheryl Taylor for the help I have received in shepherding the book through the production process. Sealy Yates, my highly capable agent, and Tom Thompson of his staff, have provided me with more help and inspiration than perhaps they know.

INTRODUCTION

Politics, politics. Where these days can we find refuge from it? Politics, along with the politicians who perpetrate it, permeates almost the whole of modern life. Laws, regulations, and judicial decisions prescribe in singular and unprecedented detail the steps we are bound to take, the paths we are supposed to walk. And with what effects? Has the science of democratic government made us happy, safe, and fulfilled? A random glance at the headlines, a conversation in passing, is enough to suggest otherwise.

A journalist who has spent his whole professional life reporting or commenting on politics might easily find himself at a loss. Is not government supposed to solve, or at the very least palliate, our major problems? Surely that's the impression we've received (from politicians, at least). Yet human beings go right on maiming, murdering, and maligning each other.

In latter times there has risen to the top of public concerns what might be called the Moral Question. Oh, we talk (and no doubt always will) of balanced budgets, welfare, taxes, environmental policy, national defense. But so, too, in these times of once-unimaginable luxury and technological achievement, we note the decay of the family, the increase in illegitimate births, the multiplication of vicious, cold-blooded crimes, and the growing indifference to the whole idea that some things are irrevocably "right," whereas others are just as irrevocably "wrong." The very concept of right and wrong is quaint to our ears, like the tinkle of a Grecian lyre.

Therapeutic government's manipulation of the social nerves and muscles has not taken away our assorted aches and pains. On the contrary, it may have made some of them worse. A well-seasoned observer of the political process can do no more than shake his head. Then, again, he *can* do more—provided his professional curiosity remains alive. Are political questions less than we political commentators have made them out to be? Are moral questions more? Such matters are worth careful examination. In turn this leads to still more momentous questions. Among these: What is morality, anyway? And whatever it may or may not be, what has it to do with the price of eggs in Arkansas?

What follows is an essay on morality in late, exceedingly late, twentieth-century America. Not for a long time have we as a society talked diligently and searchingly about the rightness of one kind of human behavior versus the wrongness of an opposite kind of behavior. Such an enterprise may seem to many twentieth-century readers joyless: morality viewed as corset, if not straitjacket. Nothing of the sort! The human enterprise, for all the tragedy in which it comes wrapped, is at its core a joyous one. Our obsession with political solutions to perceived difficulties may have obscured this insight.

The reader, at the outset of a journey such as this one, is entitled to know a bit about the would-be guide who stands clearing his throat, practicing his local pronunciations. Why would he turn from politics to the contemplation of morality? The answer is strongly implied in what has been said above: The political solution is at, or near, exhaustion. The time to move *beyond* (though without abandoning) mere politics is clearly upon us.

So, then—who is the author to stand here bold as brass, talking of morality (other people's as well as his own)? Is he unusually moral and correct in his personal life? Does he put the devil to flight whenever that dark personage hovers round, which is all day every day?

If the author did so, this essay might prove more useful to its readers or, alternatively, more syrupy and suffocating. The author makes no claim to unusual virtue and probity. Such a claim probably would not be believed anyway. Modern folk have acquired a deep skepticism—whether healthy or unhealthy is another question—regarding claimants to virtue. They have watched too many of these, in the religious as in the political sphere, crawl down from the heights to wallow in the mud pits.

An essay on morality should not be confused with a sermon—a grand "go-ye-therefore." No religious body, including his own, has ordained the author to waggle accusing fingers from the pulpit. His interest lies, rather, in analysis and prescription. An assessment of late-twentieth-century morality is a large undertaking, for which journalists have no better credentials than anyone else (save one, perhaps: employment circumstances that render curiosity something other than a leading cause of death among cats!).

Nor is our journey together essentially a religious pilgrimage. The author, a regularly practicing member of a large Christian communion, reverent, respecting the Bible and convinced concerning the creeds, must be explicit about the openness of the invitation. There is no "straight gate" here through which only "the religious" may pass. The author's conviction is that morality is best and most easily understood as a reflection of the relationship between Creator and created beings. On the other hand, the record shows that skeptics and nonbelievers are capable of exemplary moral behavior. (A sadder segment of the record reveals some self-proclaimed religious believers as less creditable, less loving, than many whom they castigate.)

From the moment he commenced this book, the author saw his audience as consisting of both the religious and the non-, or perhaps not-yet, religious. We are all in this together, are we not?—wanderers in a dangerous land with few guardrails or well-lit lamps, where necessarily we keep breaking our legs and our hearts. The replacement of those guardrails, the relighting of those lamps is the task before us—larger even than the balancing of the federal budget, timelier than all the information superhighways human reason can chart.

PART ONE

In Flight from Morality

Let's face it.
America is sick.
　　　　—Ann Landers, June 1993

✩ ✩ ✩

CHAPTER ONE

Pizza—and Death

A summer Saturday. Freshly brewed coffee and a light breeze brushing the barely opened pages of the newspaper. Whatever is going on in the world?

Politics, business, sports, and on page 33A a color photograph of the kind of teenage boy who in times past would have been called by his elders "clean-cut." He looks to be about fourteen years old, fifteen at most, and wears a neat white T-shirt with western motif on the front. Wiry brown hair bristles atop his head in the manner of President Bill Clinton's. The trace of a smile brightens an agreeable face. Just a normal, all-American-looking kid who is in the paper—why?

As the reader's eye journeys from photograph to caption, his heart beats faster. Something is hugely amiss. Donnie Mayo—that is the all-American name of the all-American boy—"was mutilated by childhood friends for vengeance, police say. The gang members used a hammer to push one eye back into his skull and flattened his nose into his face.

They did it because Donnie had beaten a gang member so badly he had to be hospitalized."

Donnie of the all-American looks, himself a near murderer? Cruelly executed at too young an age even to qualify for a driver's license? The reader on this mild morning knows he has glanced involuntarily into the abyss—and that baleful presences have stared back at him.

Recoiling, the reader runs his eye farther down the page, only to encounter fresh horrors. A pizza deliveryman, arriving in broad daylight at a suburban apartment complex with a security gate, has been attacked, robbed, and brutally beaten by the teenagers who placed the order. Leaving the man to die, the teenagers eat the pizzas and guzzle the drinks, then drive the deliveryman's truck from Texas to Illinois, where a few days later police catch up with them. All these exertions net the robbers sixty dollars. Of course, the pizza and drinks were free.

Callous violence always startles, the more so when violent acts are committed coolly, casually, and without visible sign of remorse on the perpetrators' part.

"What can we do this afternoon?"

"Let's rob a pizza deliveryman."

Thus the trap opens and closes. Nearly as startling as the pizza plotters' casual violence is their indifference to the laws of self-preservation. The young predators have given the pizza company their address and phone number. The police are certain to reel them in—but perhaps not for a day or two. Meanwhile, there is the thrill of attempted murder—and the aroma of fresh-baked mozzarella.

America is sick, Ann Landers declares. Yet for all the columnist's years of experience and gifts of observation, she tells us nothing more than we have known all along. Stories like the aforementioned—bear traps for an unwary reader—drive home over and over the gruesome point that flagrant disrespect for one's fellow human beings is widespread and expanding in these ember years of the twentieth century and second millennium of the Christian era.

The violence such stories call to our attention is bad enough. But something else shocks equally: the comfortable amorality of the violent, their increasingly common indifference to once well-lighted boundaries of personal conduct. The old borders were familiar enough: On this side, behavior in accordance with ancient and respected norms, passed down from generation to generation; on the other side, behavior that no decent society could possibly condone. This is no longer so in America, as we are reminded with awful frequency and rapidity. The lights along the moral boundary line have flickered out one by one. Greater and greater numbers of our fellow citizens have no idea such lines of demarcation ever existed. Our culture is beginning to harvest the deadly fruits of their ignorance.

This matter goes beyond physical brutality and violence. It extends to the conditions that produce violence. What are those conditions? Not long ago many sociologists and politicians commonly replied: poverty, discrimination, lack of economic opportunity. Considerable numbers still hew to that line, if not always with the zealous conviction of twenty years ago. After all, the federal government's unprecedented attack on poverty and racism during the past quarter of a century has coincided with a huge surge in crime and disorder among the poor.

What actually has changed is the way late-twentieth century Americans think about aggressive, antisocial behavior. Under the moral dispensation that prevailed as recently as thirty years ago, the mere thought of participating in such actions excited horror and disgust. On what basis does one make this assertion? On the basis of that era's rate of violent crime: a mere sixth of what it is today. The expected reply of most Americans then to a proposal of moral mayhem was, simply, "No—it's wrong!"

The importance of this intangible barrier to crime and aggression is impossible to overstate—especially now that it is so low almost anyone can hurdle it, children included.

In these strained, stressful times, we talk of the need for jail cells, handcuffs, and guns. These things are needful, all right—but only secondarily. Social peace and order depend far less on the tools of law enforcement than on the citizenry's inbred respect for "right" behavior and its corresponding opposition to behavior considered "wrong." Even policemen on every corner could not contain the impulses of a citizenry convinced there is no morality, no web of duties and obligations to others. Conversely, a community persuaded of the moral law's urgency needs only minimal policing. Where there is moral conviction—and where it guides to a large degree the lives of most citizens—people are free and secure. Where such conviction falters, people are slaves to the chain lock, the peephole, and the nervous, backward glance at night.

Civilization and immorality are fundamentally incompatible. We deceive ourselves if we imagine a commonwealth in which the rules are made up daily on an ad hoc basis—acknowledged when convenient, yet thrown out when they pinch and restrain. This is no commonwealth at all, we come to realize, but rather a moral (or amoral) jungle.

It would be rash to say that the America of the 1990s is already such a jungle. Yet it would be silly to deny the reality of the vines of immorality that coil through our streets, homes, and offices, attaching themselves to whatever and whomever they can, wherever they can, and perpetually shooting forth fresh tendrils.

A full-blown moral crisis is surely upon us—hence this book, whose topic is morality and whose point is threefold: (1) We cannot live without morality. Yet (2) having failed in our own time to cultivate moral awareness, we are reaping the deadly consequences. Although, (3) we have still the power to reverse those consequences—if we truly wish to, and if we work at the task with persistence and courage.

Before we proceed, some spade work is in order. We modern Americans may have become corrupt—but how corrupt when viewed against the vast backdrop of world history? The most corrupt civilization ever? Second most? Third? These are interesting (if fruitless) questions. There is nothing new under the sun, least of all the pastime of yearning for the past. Niccolo Machiavelli observed in his *Discourses* that "men ever praise the olden time and find fault with the present." The Old Testament teems with brooding commentary upon the unsatisfactory behavior of the chosen people. "Everyone is an hypocrite and an evildoer, and every mouth speaks folly," declares Isaiah (9:17), without conscious hyperbole. An accurate maxim for our day? We do well to remind ourselves that the prophet spoke these words more than 2,000 years ago.

In our own century, moods of deep pessimism have alternated with that rapturous optimism for which Americans are famous. More often, the prevailing sentiment is that the country is going to the dogs. Yet is this to say we'll never get there? It hardly seems sensible to suppose that because things have been bad before they cannot become worse. The condition of American culture, by any measurement, is demonstrably more discouraging than was the case barely thirty years ago.

"Over the last few decades," former U.S. Education Secretary William J. Bennett wrote in 1993, "we have experienced substantial social regression. Today the forces of social decomposition are challenging—and in some instances, overwhelming—the forces of social composition." What Bennett calls his Index of Leading Cultural Indicators shows that since 1960 "there has been a 560 percent increase in violent crime; more than a 400 percent increase in illegitimate births; a quadrupling in divorce rates; a tripling of the percentage of children living in single-parent homes; more than a 200 percent increase in the teenage suicide rate; and a drop of almost 80 points in the S.A.T. [Scholastic Aptitude Test] scores. Modern-day social pathologies, at least great parts of them, have gotten worse."[1] There is plenty here to frighten us—but likewise to challenge and stimulate us. In either case, the arduous journey toward moral recovery can be postponed no longer. The hour is late.

Would Donnie of the all-American looks have savagely beaten his friend, and suffered in return a savage death, had our society taught more unflinchingly the principles of moral rectitude? Might a hapless pizza deliveryman have been spared pain and humiliation at the hands of his own customers? We don't know. We do know, or can easily surmise, the depth of our society's timidity and confusion in moral matters—the murky nature of its witness as to right and wrong, good and evil, truth and falsehood.

The law of the jungle slowly but effectively supersedes the law of God and man. It is time to find another way—a way back.

CHAPTER TWO

The Owner's Manual

Spreading the alarm about the ongoing consequences of moral failure is easy enough. When it comes to resurrecting respect for morality itself, that's another matter entirely.

To defenders of the old moral order, the twentieth century has liberally ladled out wormwood, gall, and intellectual contempt of the sort that H. L. Mencken popularized in his extraordinary journal, *The American Mercury*. "A moralist," Mencken informed the novelist Theodore Dreiser, "is one who holds that every human act must be either right or wrong, and that 99 percent of them are wrong."

During the 1992 presidential campaign, Vice President Dan Quayle observed with a certain reckless defiance, "I know it is not fashionable to talk about moral values." Just how unfashionable moral values had become, no one could have divined at that moment. For his mild reproof of a popular television character who had just borne a baby out of wedlock, Quayle ruefully discovered himself under assault on late-night talk shows and in op-ed columns. The

The Owner's Manual **9**

television character herself, in a subsequent episode, made great sport of her supposed tormentor.

"Morality"—a benign and useful word in our grandparents' or great-grandparents' day—has in our own time acquired the musty odor of the attic. One is almost afraid to touch it; it might crumble, like the brittle, yellowed pages of the novels from which our forebears took instruction and pleasure.

Morality, as it is commonly understood today, binds and pinches, whereas modern culture seems bent wholly on joyous, bursting liberation from restraint. Moralists, as our society sees them, are those dreary, sober-faced folk whose company no joyous, emancipated denizen of the twentieth century could endure for more than a few stifling moments. Moralists are forever poking their long noses into other people's business, telling them what to do and how to live. Liberated people, by contrast, are willing for each inhabitant of our free culture to "do his own thing" without reference to other people's "preferences."

As it happens, the common understanding of morality is almost wholly false: a stereotype, an artificial construct. This understanding, nonetheless, is what has to be overcome before moral reconstruction may occur. There is no use saying "Do what is right" if the culture repudiates, as ours largely does, the very notion of norms and standards that obligate us all.

What *is* morality, then, if it is not a set of rigid rules concocted by unpleasant people so as to inflict on others the frustration they feel in their own shrunken lives? Could it be called, in more neutral language, a code of conduct? Perhaps. A kind of behavioral code exists in all cultures. One does, or doesn't do, certain things. Every Western movie addict used to know, for instance, the so-called "code of the West": Keep conversation to a monosyllabic minimum, never duck a challenge to fight, and refrain from kissing the girl until her ranch has been duly saved. Such rules obviously aren't very transferrable. Thus, a code of business ethics is designed for the workplace; in the home, different situations require different guidelines.

The point is that we cannot view morality as a set of social prescriptions, whether formally or informally enforced and subject to dramatic change. Codes indeed can change, along with circumstances. When a new order arises, we simply change the code—formally or informally. On such occasions we talk less about what is right than about what is useful, or, as the case may be, what is broadly acceptable to the majority of those concerned.

Not so with morality. We find in the moral order the expected depth and thickness of rules: no murder, no assault, no thievery, and so on. The difference is, not one such rule can rightly be called a reflection of time or place or circumstance or, for that matter, popular approval. The standards for moral judgment are altogether higher than that. Let us say a culture of crooks desired to legalize robbery of the tax-paying public, and that it enlisted in this effort the full apparatus of democracy: public meetings, debates, ballot boxes. Let us say, too, that the effort met with success. Would this legitimize a formerly illegitimate activity? Clearly, it would not. Thievery under any name would remain thievery. (We have seen endeavors of just this sort, in fact, as when the Russian Bolsheviks, circa 1918, made robbery an instrument of state policy without alleviating the moral horror their depredations produced.)

It is time to pose the question toward which this discussion has pointed: Just what is morality, anyway? If not a code or a statute, what then?

Morality, rightly understood, is *a set of propositions about human nature:* who we are, where we came from, where we are bound, how we ought to conduct ourselves on the journey. From these propositions flow the code or rules— guidelines for enacting our role as members of the human family. The rules point back to our nature, telling us in essence that if this is who we are, then here is what we must do about it. If a particular action harmonizes with our nature, then such an action must be, in common parlance, *right*. An action at odds with that nature—one that is dangerous or harmful to it—is *wrong*. This means that morality is never arbitrary, never the result of individual or local perception. Its roots lie deep in our nature.

The commonness of that nature is what makes morality common. It is not yours, not mine, but *ours corporately*. We are all in this together, we wayfaring, wandering humans. As it happens, not all humans relish this understanding. "Get your morality out of my face!" is a statement heard often today. There are several things worth noticing about this posture. One is the assumption that the offending morality is the personal property of the party wielding it, a thing with no more significance than a dishwasher, a dress, or a municipal bond. The morality in question is "yours"—not mine, not the culture's, the country's, the church's, the service club's. Rather, it is yours—pertaining to you and lacking relevance to me. There is no overarching standard of belief—nothing we necessarily see alike.

This brings up another implication: Just as there are many dishwashers and dresses, so conceivably there are many moralities, "yours" being just one of them. Maybe I have one, too—as may my neighbor, my barber, my employer. These different moralities may have as many areas of agreement as they do of disagreement. The point to notice would be their variety and distinctiveness.

There is a further point worth noticing: In my indignation upon finding "your" morality thrust suddenly into my face, I bridle. Why? Would my reaction be the same if, say, our difference of viewpoint concerned Mexican restaurants or television newscasts? We could agree on these subjects to differ respectfully. Yet when morality enters the equation, intellectual private-property sensors emit a banshee's wail.

The truth is that morality—yours, mine, anyone else's—inherently limits choices in life. Or, if you will, it guides our choices. Even this hopeful formulation runs contrary to the modern spirit, which affirms the right to endless self-expression. What happens when you advertise a little too zealously your view of how I should live? You menace my right to free choice. You suggest, subtly and gingerly, that I live as you do. Well, what if I don't care to? How do you know in the first place what is good or prudent or just or kind for me? And if you don't know, what do I want with *your* opinion? *Get your morality out of my face!*

Does it become clearer now what is going on? Morality, formerly a good word, is seen as a bad one—if not out-and-out bad, at least divisive, a fragmenting force in society, pitting neighbor against neighbor, sibling against sibling, child against parent. All of which flies in the face of the presumption noted above—the presumption of our common humanity. If our humanity is common, why can't we acknowledge it?

In fact, we do. There is a vogue for humanity conceived as a worldwide, multicultural sea of faces. We swim in it daily. The Reverend John Donne's famous lines, "No man is an island, entire of itself; every man is a piece of the continent, a part of the main," are famous precisely because they express with concrete sublimity the post-World War II conviction that ours in fact is One World. The victorious Allied Forces in 1946 tried and executed Nazi leaders for crimes against humanity—crimes, that is, against people whose looks and language might differ from the Allies' own, but who shared all other human properties—faces, hearts, lives. The United Nations Charter since that era has "guaranteed" specific human rights. Yet our common humanity runs deeper than mere legal codes. Whenever there is calamity, here or abroad, the tingle of human sympathy rushes through human veins distant from the crisis site. As tokens of fellow-feeling, we donate money and clothes to the victims.

Often in the modern age, patriotism meets with verbal attack, as though devotion to one's native land showed disdain for others' cultures and homelands. American universities are adopting curricula that require the study and appreciation of non-Western cultures. Foreign-language studies flourish here as never before. All of this shows that modern Americans are not totally compartmentalized, each living in a state of self-absorption.

Still, something is lacking in the human concept of humanity. It is the sense of *common obligation.* In other words, if we have similar rights as human beings, so must we have similar duties and obligations. We do not share this sense today—which helps to explain the modern moral mess.

Whence comes such a sense? From an accompanying sense of *common origin.* James Q. Wilson points to gender and culture as shapers of (to borrow his book title) the "moral sense," so that morality, in origin, is "parochial and easily blunted by even trivial differences between what we think of as familiar and what we define as strange." It is a useful but easily exhausted insight. Gender and culture take us back only so far. Whence gender? Whence culture? Sociology affords only suggestions. Religion, on the other hand, knows nothing of tentativeness. It declares boldly, with conviction, what happened. It says that, in the beginning, God "happened."

We begin now to wade in deep waters. The citizen of a secular inclination—who takes his philosophy from the newsmagazines, the lecture podium, or the talk shows—may exclaim at this point, "Jumping Jupiter, what have I walked into, a church service?" Not so. The author is a journalist, not a theologian. He asks only for a mind open to the proposition that passing years may not have rendered irrelevant the once-familiar framework of moral discourse, stamped with the name of God.

Consider the religious view of mankind. It is that we are divinely wrought, for a divinely ordained purpose. In the beginning was no gender, no culture—just the sovereign will of God who, according to written, carefully conserved testimony, said, "Let us make man in our image, after our likeness: and let them have dominion over the fish of the sea, and over the fowl of the air, and over the cattle, and over all the earth, and over every creeping thing that creepeth upon the earth. So God created man in his own image; in the image of God created he him; male and female created he them."[1] At this point we have gender, but only in a rudimentary sense; as for culture, no one has heard of it.

Yet precisely here begins the moral law—mankind as the creation of God, subject to the Creator's commands. These arise instantly. Hardly has the new man located a limpid stream in which to admire himself before the Creator lays obligations upon him: "Be fruitful, and multiply, and replenish the earth, and subdue it . . ." It turns out there are negative as well as affirmative duties: "Of the tree of the knowledge of good and evil, thou shalt not eat of it."[2]

Why such commands? And why not? On one level, because the Creator issued them, and no back talk, if you please. (In like manner, virtually every parent recognizes "Because I said so!" as the ultimate weapon in the disciplinary arsenal.) But there is more to the matter than the legal injunctions so many moderns find objectionable in the moral code. Why was the created being to obey his Creator? Because obedience would align him with the purposes his Creator had in mind for him—such purposes as multiplication and replenishment of the population.

The book of Genesis is a tricky, even dangerous, narrative to pour into the open ear of a culture that for over a century has been accustomed to hearing the story either mythologized or dismissed altogether. The author's purpose is not to debate the authenticity of the narrative; it is, rather, to illuminate the question of human origins. Did God create us, or did he not?

Let us say, for the sake of argument, he did not. Let us say instead that humanity erupted somehow and took shape without obligation to allegedly divine beings. Let us declare God, or gods, irrelevant to moral purposes. There would be nothing new in this. Entire ethical systems have been based largely on human intuition and perception. The Stoics and

Epicureans needed no divine ordinances on which to ground their respective ethics. Nor did Immanuel Kant, whose enormously influential system glorifies human reason. H. L. Mencken based his own "private code," which he deemed "superior to that of most Christians," on personal honor. The man of honor, such as the Sage of Baltimore deemed himself, was guided by his innate sense of decency. One could call each of these codes restrictive, as surely they were for their adherents. Mencken, for example, never would have mugged a little old lady; his sense of honor would have interposed itself had the temptation arisen.

Yet for those who subject themselves to no code save the laws of the United States (and not always even that code), the variety of ethical systems available in these times is liberating. There is something for every taste. Consumer sovereignty has been transported from the economic marketplace into the moral realm. All manner of "lifestyles" and possibilities open up. This chaotic state of affairs overrules the possibility of any code which compels, however lovingly, consistent acts of obedience. Obedience to what, and to whom? Where does ultimate authority reside?

Under humanly contrived systems of ethics, the individual is sovereign. This sounds quite comfortable until one reckons with the consequences. These consequences might be described, in the terminology of Thomas Hobbes three centuries ago, as the war of all against all, lasting until the individual with the largest, sharpest sword stalks into the arena, commanding allegiance and enforcing order. The vision is as unattractive as it is hauntingly familiar. We have glimpsed it in the lurid fires of Los Angeles in 1992. We have heard the cries and yelps of the mobs as they replaced the order of civility and commerce with one of aggression, violence, and murder.

So we take up the contrary alternative—that, as our civilization has affirmed from the beginning (though with diminishing conviction), God created man in his own image. Divine origin makes humanity subject to divine oversight. If God created man, it follows that he had a purpose in doing so. It follows equally that a Creator's purpose takes precedence over any that the creature might devise for his or her own satisfaction. (In no known realm do creator and creature function as equals; always the former outranks the latter.)

And what is the Creator's purpose? There are various answers. In the Jewish tradition, the One God has chosen Israel out of all nations to be God's "peculiar people," reverent and obedient to him. Upon this claim the Christian tradition builds. Owing to the death and resurrection of Jesus Christ, the final destiny of man is heaven—or, as man himself wills, hell. In heaven, one's human nature, conferred at birth, achieves fulfillment; in hell, it meets frustration.

So, is morality about "getting to heaven"? That is one way of putting it. Certainly, in the Christian tradition, salvation has less to do with outward compliance than with inward faith. At the same time, that tradition holds that good works proceed from honest faith. The point really lies elsewhere, however; it is that particular actions and abstinences are incumbent upon those humans who would fulfill, not fight against, their God-given nature.

Morality has been called the "owner's manual for the human body." Owners' manuals we know about. We know we are to change a car's oil every 3,000 miles or so; we are to maintain brakes and tire pressure and to perform other operations agreeable with the principles on which the car has been constructed. The performance of these various operations should ensure the smooth functioning and long life of the vehicle. It is much the same with that infinitely more complex and generally more perplexing structure, the human being. We humans are to do particular things for the maintenance of self and community: deal fairly with others; refrain from inflicting injury; treat spouses with honor and consideration; take responsibility for the well-being of children; observe manmade laws. No one of these principles is startling. All are (or once were) ordinary expectations, like oil changes at regular intervals. Performing them guarantees at a minimum that the streets will be safe, the home peaceful, the government honest, the workplace just and equitable. Such a state of affairs may bore some of our fellow citizens to tears, assuming they enjoy the flash and sizzle of a society frying in its own juices. The number of these citizens, one hopes, is small.

We have yet to note one final characteristic of a religiously based moral law. While one hates to label it "socially useful," it is precisely that. That characteristic is the moral law's *hierarchial nature*. It comes to us from above—that is, from God, who is above (whether spatially or in some other exalted sense) the totality of his creation.

Always the religious gaze is not sideways but upward. The Creator God speaks; his creations listen (or commonly find they wish they had). The locus of true moral authority is (if one objects to the word *heaven*) wherever God abides.

Without authority, what then? Back to Hobbes and to Los Angeles we go, different dogmatisms snapping and snarling at each other; no one "lifestyle" more right than another, now that our culture has mostly closed down the old moral checkpoints, whose directional signs pointed upward. Everyone pretty much runs his own show, nor does the culture feel bound to recommend any particular show as most satisfying or compelling. In fact, it grows increasingly unrealistic to speak of *the* culture. How would anyone define American culture today apart from its generalized commitment to popular expression? Where is the culture's sense of purpose? Does it hope to progress anywhere in particular, or just to let nature take its course?

The story of the twentieth century is largely that of the steady erosion of allegiance to a religiously based standard of morality, and its replacement by a standard that is in fact no standard at all but, rather, an amalgam of individual insights and judgments. This is why the story of the twentieth century is one of unprecedented bloodshed and brutality, strangely mixed with episodes of human concern for others—orphans taken in, victims of disaster sheltered, victims of oppression rescued and vindicated.

These last manifestations seem to bar the otherwise open pathway to despair. The fabled generosity and idealism of the ordinary American live on amid gunshots and sirens. This should not coax us into complacency; it should remind us of all we can be, when what we do fits who we are.

✯ ✯ ✯

CHAPTER THREE

A Short History of Twentieth-Century Morals

... But, then, who were we, say, thirty years ago? A people of laudable virtue, whose ideals the present generation should try harder to imitate? What if the Beatles and Beach Boys and Kennedys were once again our popular idols? Would not that be a wonderful thing? Maybe then we would not be running around hijacking automobiles, aborting unborn babies, and what not.

Such an inference—which seeps through conservative punditry frequently—goes farther than the evidence justifies. Who were we, anyway, in the early sixties? A people journeying toward the nineties, but with considerable ground left to cover. At that, we had covered considerable ground since the start of the century, a time of attitudes so unimaginably stern by modern standards that we can scarcely believe our ancestors put up with what they did in the name of decency and dignity. But they did. Alas, their children did not, still less their grandchildren. As for their great-great-grandchildren—well, what our forebears would make of it all, we really don't wish to speculate.

Deploring the later, as distinguished from the earlier, 1960s is in vogue among conservative social critics. This is hardly unreasonable, considering the disruptions the decade produced: campus violence, Jerry Rubin's hyperbolic injunction to "kill your parents," the counterculture, welfare as a way of life, and the downgrading and belittling of standards across the board—moral, religious, cultural, educational, literary. Of the trashy-libidinous novels cherished in the early sixties, the humorist P. J. O'Rourke writes wistfully, "In three decades we've gone from not being able to talk about such things to not being able to shut up about them."[1] The scholar Myron Magnet credits (or rather, discredits) the utopian social experiments of the sixties with leading the poor to ruin—in short, convincing them they were victims and thereby sucking out their dignity and self-respect.

Yet what has gone wrong in America cannot be traced solely to the sixties. No one compelled the Americans of that era to behave as they did. They behaved so because they wanted to. The question is *Why* did they want to? Let us remember, moreover, that the children of the sixties mostly were born in the forties and raised in the fifties, supposedly the decades of innocent Howdy Doody values; when Robert Young, playing Jim Anderson on "Father Knows Best," hung up his hat in the front hall and proceeded with patience and good cheer to unravel the ephemeral difficulties that Princess, Bud, and Kitten were encountering. Gentle Dave Garroway, on the "Today Show," raised his hand and wished us "Peace." Our respect for what we regard in retrospect as traditional values ought to have stopped the sixties in their tracks. It did not. "If we accept the premise of 'family values' advocates," writes John Attarian, "that the child is father to the man, then the sixties mayhem proves that something was wrong with millions of American families in the fifties. . . ."[2] Maybe it was. Certainly adults then regarded the music and dancing styles of the day as vulgar (although a recent article in a noted conservative journal celebrated doo-wop music's "traditional themes and vocal harmony"). Then there were juvenile delinquents ("J.D.'s," in the parlance of the day), with their greased hair, leather jackets, and growing propensity to defy laws as well as social conventions. They were a less clean-cut species than the seventies musical "Grease" depicted—though collectively they couldn't hold a candle to the inner-city gangs of the '90s.

There were softer, subtler signs of cultural loosening: the abstract expressionist style in painting and the "beat" culture, with its ethic of disengagement and oriental modes of reflection. One should not say such phenomena "caused" the sixties; rather, they fed the social currents that ultimately overflowed their banks.

No, blaming the blameworthy sixties does not suffice. We need a longer, broader view. What has been the hallmark of this century as a whole? And of the century before that? The constant, ongoing relaxation of authority. We need to examine this matter carefully. It is the key to everything.

Authority, like morality, has acquired a bad name in the 1990s. It is no wonder. The two concepts are interrelated and often interdependent; our view of one directly influences our view of the other. Let us remember: morality is no mere set of prescriptions and directives—do this, do that, do the other. Morality is, rather, *a set of propositions about who we humans are, with accompanying guidelines for the proper care and maintenance of our nature.* Overzealous moralists in time past have tended to talk as though the directives themselves mattered more than the consequences of following or not following them. The letter of the law obscured the code's inner rationale. The author's mother recalls how certain Protestant ministers in the small Texas town where she grew up in the 1920s came close to defining morality as the total avoidance of card playing, dancing, moviegoing, and like temptations of the flesh. No doubt there were other sins to be faced, such as pride, but these were harder to spot and confront than was a gangly high schooler lounging in the balcony of the local picture palace.

Yet the dismal experience of the succeeding seven decades has made clear the dangers inherent in too neatly severing morality and authority. The very maintenance of propositions about human nature depends on authority. Someone (or some Other) must set forth the propositions—show them to us, explain their working, outline the indicated response. When on receiving the explanation, we nod understandingly, we acknowledge an authority outside ourselves. In doing so we say, in effect, this thing is larger than we are.

Yet herein lies the problem: For authority to receive acknowledgment, there first must exist the disposition, public or private, to acknowledge it. A society with a high view of authority's legitimacy is ready enough to say, yes, this is right, this is true. It is different with a society increasingly convinced the only right judgment is individual judgment. Ours is such a society.

The European Enlightenment—that pivotal intellectual movement of the past two centuries, exemplified by Voltaire, Diderot, Rousseau, and Hume—reached the colonists in America apparently with as much power as it had reached their relatives in Europe. Benjamin Franklin and Thomas Jefferson, both of whom were to represent this country at the Enlightenment's geographical fountainhead, Paris, were among the movement's eager disciples. The premise of the movement, Crane Brinton notes graphically, was the substitution "for the *transcendental,* God-determined Christian otherworldly heaven a this-world *transformed* by human reason guiding human action into . . . well, the phrase is inadequate, but 'a heaven on earth' will have to do."[3]

The emphasis on reason cannot be stated too strongly. Humanity was capable, in the view of Enlightenment philosophers, of working out for itself the grounds of being and behaving. Human brainpower and attainments, they claimed, had demonstrated as much, and could demonstrate even more once our habit of reflexive submission to Deity had passed.

One can grasp easily the political implications of such a movement. Suddenly, sovereigns and potentates were answerable to the people. The new perception brought France's worm-eaten old regime crashing down in 1789, amid carnage and gore, and contributed as well to the English colonists' exasperation with King George III.

America seemed uniquely suited for a movement such as the Enlightenment. In a newly settled land of unlimited possibilities (and seemingly limitless boundaries), humanity could start virtually afresh. The dead hand of the old order could be pried at last from civilization's windpipe. This was not just bracing stuff—it was intoxicating. "Bliss was in that dawn to be alive," Wordsworth wrote in recollection of the early stages of the French Revolution. The American colonists, applying scissors to the mother country's apron strings, felt some of the same exhilaration.

Amid those momentous happenings, the vertical view of humanity and its place in the universe began yielding to a horizontal view. No longer would the people of the eighteenth century look "up" for inspiration; they would look sideways—toward family, friends, colleagues.

"Up," "down," "sideways"—the terms convey not just direction, but attitude and disposition. A sense of God's "aboveness" (not to be confused as it often is with aloofness) is the viewpoint—or, if you will, the worldview—of classical Christianity and Judaism. "O come, let us worship and *bow down:* let us *kneel* before the LORD our maker," enjoins the psalmist (emphasis mine). He underlines humanity's irremediable position in a passage that continues, "For he is our God; and we are the people of his pasture, and the sheep of his hand."[4] A text of this character leaves little room for doubt that Creator and created do not meet on terms of social equality—bosom buddies, pals for life. The sense of awe that permeates the encounter between man and God is entirely on man's part.

At this point, an obvious question surfaces: How does the vertical relationship affect the functioning of the parties involved in the relationship—One higher, the other lower? Just as one would suppose, the higher party commands, the lower obeys. Such is the idea, at least.

So it has been in religion much more than in politics. The king, though he ruled an earthly domain, bore to the Almighty the same relationship as did tailors, farmers, and carters—one of abject dependency. Obedience was built into the whole relationship of man to God—joyful obedience, in no way resembling the secular terror that many mortal rulers have imposed on their trembling people. If the Almighty had his terrifying side, especially in relationship to those who disobeyed him, had he not reached out in incomprehensible love, offering his only Son as a sacrifice for us in our helpless state of sin? The Christian culture affirmed as much.

There would come a time in religious deliberation when the accusation arose that some of those who represented the mind of God to his people were not always reliable messengers—that too often they had a personal stake in how the message was imparted and received. This suspicion, which became sharp at the time of the Reformation, actually did not subvert the underlying principle of divine sovereignty. If anything, it persuaded some to cast their eyes higher than the earthly ministers with whom they dealt, and to contemplate for themselves, as far as they could, the heavenly throne.

God's authority was safe with those who understood the essential verticality of the relationship. But the understanding was not to endure. Today, generally speaking, we are horizontalists—in practice, if not in theory. Authority cuts little ice with us. I see my neighbor's judgment as no better on philosophical grounds than my own, and I expect he regards his own judgment in just the same way. We are good democrats.

Democracy, indeed, is what it all comes down to—political theory transferred to the cultural and moral realm. The transfer in retrospect may seem regrettable, but it likely was inevitable. A nation whose statutes and political habits are based on the participation of the sovereign voters has no right, even in the midst of crisis, to look down its nose at democracy. Few if any of the founding fathers would applaud the lengths to which democratic theory has carried the United States: universal adult suffrage, with "adult" defined as eighteen years or older; property ownership disallowed as a benchmark of "fitness" for the franchise; voter registration, under recent federal legislation, made possible at the time and place one registers a motor vehicle; and so on. Nonetheless, this is what we now mean by political democracy.

In most of its manifestations, democracy has well served the United States. "I have been in full harmony all my life," Winston Churchill told the U.S. Congress in 1941, "with the tides which have flowed on both sides of the Atlantic against privilege and monopoly, and I have steered confidently toward the Gettysburg ideal of 'government of the people, by the people, for the people.'"[5] If democracy spewed up on occasion unfruitful or even wicked rulers, the means of ousting and replacing them remained wide open. And if universal suffrage disappointed its promoters by failing to involve virtually everyone in the political process, the nation prided itself in the wisdom and patience of "the common man."

The question is whether the ideals useful in the political sphere should be carried over into the moral sphere. So all men are equal? What about all ideas, viewpoints, codes, standards, outlooks? Do all carry the same weight in our political democracy? Clearly not. There remains even today a consensus as to certain basics. No civilization has ever ratified, for example, the ideal of thievery (though foes of the personal income tax maintain our own society has done so!). A "principled" murderer—a fictional Raskolnikov or a real-life Nathan Leopold—would receive short shrift from the courts (though the lobby that resists and drags out the process of execution is vigorous and vocal). Very well. This does not mean the narrower, stricter moral standards of the founding fathers remain in place under our more spacious and relaxed dispensation.

The spread of the horizontal outlook in politics—every citizen's vote equal to every other's—has been infectious. The achievement of women's suffrage accompanied the start of the Jazz Age, with its speakeasies and rumble-seat sex. The civil rights movement slightly preceded the formation of the counterculture. My point is not to speak other than kindly of women's suffrage or the full realization of civil rights for blacks; it is to say that the egalitarian impulse—the horizontal view—has worked in different spheres in different ways. The point to notice is that it worked. The history of the last two centuries is one of broadening and flattening in almost every respect. Mountain peaks of authority were hacked down to scalable dimensions. The vertical, upward view of life lost favor. Horizontality prevailed.

How did this affect religion and morality? In pungent ways. God had revealed himself unmistakably as a monarch, indeed *the* monarch (e.g., "The LORD reigneth, he is clothed with majesty"—Psalm 93:1). God could be called the heavenly archetype of the princes who ruled in his stead down below. But in the earthly realm, democracy sapped the authority of kings, and a deadly European war ruined various dynasties outright. The chief monarchy remaining today, Britain's, exercises mostly cultural functions. It was not inevitable, perhaps, that as earthly monarchies waned, heavenly kingship would suffer. Yet the nineteenth century, the century of democracy, saw an upsurge in challenges to theological authority. These challenges were framed as assaults not so much on God's authority as on the authority of his worldly interpreters. Sometimes, even so, it was hard to know the difference.

The French Revolution had overthrown the Catholic Church en toto—bishops, breviaries, cathedrals. Not surprisingly, the revolutionaries enthroned in Notre Dame cathedral a more typical deity: the goddess of Reason. This was for only a short time; the bishops returned in what Reason's apostles doubtless saw as unreasonable haste. But in the years after the revolution, challenges to religious authority multiplied everywhere. Early in the nineteenth century, German biblical scholars began emphasizing less the Bible's divinely inspired quality than the perceived activity of mere humans in stitching it together from disparate manuscripts and traditions. The Bible became more and more "horizontal"—a compilation resulting from human choices. If particular humans long ago could choose regarding what the church read and believed, then particular humans in the present could bring their own insights to the Bible's interpretation.

Ralph Waldo Emerson and the New England Transcendentalists downplayed shared views of reality; they emphasized what was personal, individual. Man needed no dogma, no systems of authority, the Transcendentalists taught with considerable effect. And the evolution controversy—which today rages mostly out of view, surfacing occasionally in book reviews and courtrooms—further undermined over a period of decades the reverential status that Christians had accorded the Genesis account of Creation. As scholars convinced themselves of evolution's intellectual claims, they shook off what they saw as religion's brazen impositions. Various scholars addressed themselves to the task of searching for the "real" Jesus, who, by clear implication was someone other than the God-Man of the Gospels and Epistles.

Was all of this bad? Not necessarily. If God, as Christians affirmed, created the human mind, he necessarily had to be pleased to see that mind busy at work, applying itself to problems previously unanticipated or unappreciated. What if knowledge had stopped with Aristotle? With Newton? Yet unmistakably the neglect, if not the denigration, of authority had adverse consequences for religion. Questions formed in a spirit of piety were one thing. Questions that mocked or scorned religion were something else entirely.

These questions increased in quantity and volume as the nineteenth century advanced. There was no way to rule them out. Increasingly all inquiries, like all men, were equal—to be met with equal seriousness and to be accorded equal rights in discourse, both public and private.

It is not easy to paint a picture of the modern religious world. Not all authority has been leveled down, but on the other hand much has. Even inside a church like the Roman Catholic, with its high view of authority, there is dissent from official church teaching on moral matters. A rather self-consciously daring Episcopal bishop, John Shelby Spong, regularly challenges in his writings the authority of Scripture, especially Saint Paul's writings. This right reverend father in God rejects the Trinity, the Virgin Birth, and the bodily Resurrection of Jesus, all keystones of Christian belief. The bishop pooh-poohs their validity and importance. His own church has leveled at him not so much as a chastising finger. Other supposedly "mainstream" churches are buffeted by the same currents of thought and conviction.

The connection with morality is plain enough. To the extent that morality depends on religion (a matter we shall explore fully in subsequent chapters), it is compromised by the weak regard in which religious authority is held nowadays. Religious teaching on morality enjoys no special status in modern America. Churches are entitled to their "opinions," certainly, as are all social and cultural institutions, but no such opinions bind anyone. In fact, it would be hard to consider as binding on us such a variety of views as the churches deliver nowadays on moral questions. Modern people looking for definitive guidance on the important questions of life wander in darkness. Yet they need not wander far. There is more light than they suppose.

CHAPTER FOUR

Free Sex and
Other Delusions

An inquiry into 1990s morality necessarily commences with sex. There is no choice: In the nineties everything commences with sex, from human relationships to television talk shows. To every appearance, the society of the nineties has sex on the brain—surely a strange place to have it, as Malcolm Muggeridge observed.

A seemingly naive question arises: Just what *is* sex, anyway?

The question sounds naive because, given the constant exposure sex enjoys in our culture, there can hardly be anyone over the age of five who lacks some notion of the techniques involved. In various schools, first- and second-graders learn the tactics of sexual protection by pulling condoms over bananas. (What impression of bananas this leaves in tender minds, no one appears to have inquired.)

At every turn sex is advertised as gratification, a surefire pathway to pleasure. Commercial advertisements, often exceptionally well produced, create for hard-breathing viewers lingering associations: Product X and sleek, tanned, barely clothed bodies go together. No actual promise is implied, such as "Buy plantation shutters, and, oh, the sights you'll see through them!" Still, the soft-focus image lingers.

Likewise, sex enlivens popular entertainment. This is nothing completely new. If sex were irrelevant to the purposes of entertainment, then why, over the years, have the great majority of popular actors and actresses been people of physical comeliness? Can anyone name an unprepossessing "matinee idol"? Clara Bow, Theda Bara, Rudolph Valentino, Gloria Swanson, and Douglas Fairbanks fairly reeked sexual attraction in the silent movies. In due course, Hollywood itself created the so-called "Hays Office" (after its principle tenant, Will Hays) and charged it with setting and enforcing the moral standards to which moviegoers would be exposed. Married couples, for instance, such as Nick and Nora Charles in the "Thin Man" series, slept in single beds, making it hard for audiences to envision how they ever acquired their families. (But then, that was the point—making sex hard to envision.)

Today's movies exceed in sexual content anything the Hays Office ever could have fretted about. Nudity and acts of simulated copulation have become so commonplace they no longer excite the anxious comments they provoked in the sixties. Films with heavy sexual content are readily available on home video, and must be widely played in homes or they would not be readily available.

The sexual revolution, as we call it, began in American life in the 1920s. The images are part of folklore: rumble-seat sex, bobbed hair, short skirts, cigarettes dangling from feminine fingers. Though World War I precipitated it, the revolution would have occurred in any case as women gained access not only to the workplace and the polling booth but also to transportation.

Another pervasive factor was Dr. Freud of Vienna and his new philosophy. "Sex, it appeared, was the central and pervasive force which moved mankind," Frederick Lewis Allen wrote concerning the outlook of that frantic decade.

"Almost every human motive was attributable to it: if you were patriotic or liked the violin, you were in the grip of sex—in a sublimated form. The first requirement of mental health was to have an uninhibited sex life. If you would be well and happy, you must obey your libido."[1]

Not much of staid, conservative Victorianism survived the Roaring Twenties, but the revolution required decades to achieve the impact we see today. If divorce and illegitimacy grew incrementally, the great majority of American families remained intact. With the coming of the Depression, millions saw fleshly gratification as a square meal rather than a night of sensual abandonment. Thus the thirties reinstituted a more serious style of public propriety than had been common during the Jazz Age. Sex being sex, it remained a normal concern, but no longer one of revolutionary import. World War II, like all wars, reawakened libidinal urges that accelerated during what many now think of incorrectly as the stable fifties.

It was the sixties, however, specifically the late sixties, that took up where the twenties left off. With the sixties everything came into the open—*everything*. The new voices of the sixties—hippies, yippies, counterculturists, foes of the social order—promoted sex for sex's sake, no higher justification being necessary. "Sex in the counterculture," writes Allen J. Matusow, "did not imply love between two people, but merely gratification of the self—ecstasy through orgasm. Typical encounters in Haight-Ashbury [the San Francisco district that was headquarters for hippiedom] were one-night stands, rapists prospered, and carriers of venereal disease shared it generously."[2]

All the barriers to excess, so carefully put in place over long centuries, came down with a resounding crash. The twenties had rejoiced in adultery and premarital coupling, but the sixties were uninterested in archaic institutions like bourgeois marriage. The right to "do it"—in Jerry Rubin's graphic formulation—involved the right to do anything and everything, at any place and time, spontaneously, on any pretext or none. Homosexuality and lesbianism were perfectly fine, group sex wholesome and uplifting. Even incest had its apologists. Sex was not least a political statement—a nose-thumbing at conventional society. And there were baser purposes. Members of the radical Weatherman faction of Students for a Democratic Society used forced sexual performance to degrade and control female members.[3]

None of this is to imply that in the sixties America, with its deep religious heritage and sense of moral mission, became magically a land of libertines, the new Sodom. Millions did resist then and do so now the siren call to "do it." They simply found themselves unable to roll back the advancing tide of moral permissiveness.

The sixties inevitably ended, but its spirit of liberation had taken hold in the larger culture, which began to discover the supposed joys of liberation in all its shapes and guises. America came finally to acknowledge the prophetic summons to the higher life of gratification, first sounded in the fifties by Hugh Hefner, founder of *Playboy*. A host of Hefner imitators soon jumped into the market, many out-Hefnering "Hef" in their willingness to display the most intimate anatomical details. Pornography remains a criminal offense in America, but its legal definition is much narrower than was the case even thirty years ago.

What *is* sex? we have asked. We see it, artfully posed, in photographs. We hear of it in daily conversation and every form of media. What is it, all the same?

Traditional morality offers an answer. The answer in part is that sex is much more than we think. Sex for gratification is a part of the whole but no more than a part. The much larger part is the physical aspect of *love*—the outer expression powerfully, sublimely supplementing the inner.

To speak of love in a 1990s context is no easy thing. The language of love issues from a constant, unvarying view of the relationship between the only two sexes there are. If morality is a set of propositions about human beings—what our nature is and what fulfills that nature—then the male-female relationship clearly has moral implications. How could it be otherwise, when the relationship is so large a part of life: the cause of frightful wars, mighty deeds, petty plots, and shimmering poetry?

The male-female relationship has undergone vast changes in the past sixty or seventy years, above all in the past twenty. We hear regarding the relationship today much more of the language of political democracy than formerly: rights, opportunities, upward mobility. It shows, if nothing else, how complicated the relationship has become. Votes and careers for women have moved us far beyond mandolins in the moonlight. But there are constants, too. If man and woman are made for each other—and clearly there is no alternative viewpoint—then whatever fortifies their relationship does them honor. We have for thousands of years called this relationship marriage.

Marriage could be called the foundation of morality—the domestication of love. The first thing it does is move the couple—this man, this woman—into a fixed relationship, one defined by law, civil as well as ecclesiastical, and favored by both in most respects. (U.S. tax law discriminates inexplicably against married couples in favor of single persons.) Even in the nineties the marriage relationship is so familiar we hardly pause to think of its implications. Let us identify a few of these.

Marriage, to begin with, initiates family life. A commonplace of the nineties is that there are all sorts of families in our midst, and not just the "Ozzie and Harriet" variety (mother, father, and two or more children). Today we see single-parent families; families of two men with or without children; families of two women with or without children. And certainly it is true that less than 60 percent of American children today live with both biological parents.

We are asked to think of all these new groupings as valid—equally worthwhile expressions of human affection. Those who make this claim are resolute; there is no arguing them down. Most of them are in fact defending their own family styles. The fact remains that children issue from the sexual coming together of one man and one woman, who, in the ordinary course, are married to each other. The procreation of children is the natural outcome of most marriages. We are back to sex.

The marriage relationship of a man and a woman has other important sexual features, one of which is fetchingly described in the marriage rite of the Anglican *Book of Common Prayer:* "It [marriage] was ordained for a remedy against sin, and to avoid fornication; that such persons as have not the gift of continency might marry, and keep themselves undefiled members of Christ's body." The theological language here—"sin," "Christ's body"—may meet with stony glances from those of a nonreligious bent, but fornication is a good old word and well understood. It means sexual intercourse outside the marriage bonds. The fornicator may be married or single, male or female. The married relationship is predicated on the superiority of fidelity.

Contrary to what certain critics of moral norms have said before and still say, no reasonable person ever has branded sex "immoral" or "disgusting," a thing for animals. By pretending this is what "arbiters of morality" think, the critics descend to stereotype: old pruneraces wagging their fingers at young people expressing honest physical urges.

Of course the urges are honest; of course they are physical. The question is not sex, yes or no? (That answer is yes—of course!) The real question is, sex where? In what context? Under what auspices? Inside marriage or outside?

It is wise to frame these questions within our original premise—the definition of morality. So we ask, which of these two options is more consonant with our nature?

First, the arguments for sex within marriage. These are very old. There is nothing new to say about them. If sex is the physical expression of love, then lovers have every incentive to attach themselves permanently to each other. How better to satisfy this mutual hunger—man for woman,

woman for man—than by institutionalizing it through mutual undertaking and promise? The promise underwrites the long-term continuance of the relationship. The partners know where they stand with each other. They know, in current jargon, what their rights are. So the context is set for mutual giving, emotionally and physically.

Not that establishing such a context resolves all potential difficulties! Every married couple knows what heavy sledding marriage can be: the squabbles, the differences of viewpoint and opinion, the injured feelings, the episodes of loneliness and, most alarmingly, violence. Indeed, half of all modern marriages end in divorce. Yet how can this be, when the premise of marriage is that these two people, man and wife, love each other? A truly loving couple in the end will put aside or surmount obstacles to the fulfillment of that love. Compromises and adjustments will ensue. Bumping or gliding, the relationship will go forward.

Still, these are the liberated nineties. Sex outside of marriage is widely viewed as delightful and fulfilling. The unmarried lifestyle has gained a hold on the popular imagination. Hollywood couples such as Warren Beatty and Annette Bening exemplify its glamour. No attempt is made to pretend the relationship is other than it seems. The partners appear sometimes to take pleasure in defying "conventional morality" as they express their love outside the matrimonial domain.

What could be wrong with this? And why should it concern people not directly concerned? Such questions sound new, but in fact they are old. The questioners posit the essential equality of the married and the unmarried states. This is a suitably modern thing to do, of course, the ancient concept of verticality having fallen into the discard. But we have to ask, is this really so? Is sex essentially the same, practiced inside or outside marriage?

What remains the same is the practice, which has yielded no variations in recent memory. That is as far as it goes. Vastly different are the consequences—not the subjective consequences if you please; the objective ones, plain and demonstrable; inescapable; deadly sometimes. The topic is large. Broad treatment will not do. We must break down our discussion into discrete categories.

CHAPTER FIVE

Family Problems

America, prior to the 1960s, advertised its wholehearted support of family in the traditional sense—father, mother, and children all living under the same roof. The vision of the nineties can hardly be called uniform, but, then, that is the point: the lack of a modern "orthodoxy" regarding family relations. A diverse array of supplemental possibilities presents itself: living proudly alone; living unmarried with a mate of the opposite sex, with or without children; living with a sexual partner of the same sex; etc.

None of the "new" styles is unfamiliar to students of history. The present generation did not invent cohabitation or homosexuality or lesbianism. The specialty of the nineties is the vociferous claim that each of the aforementioned "lifestyles" is as good as all the others. What matters isn't rigid obedience to niceties enforced by the community; the important thing is the "fulfillment" one finds in this relationship or that one. All relationships have become by the gauges of the nineties equal in value. There is no hierarchy of preference, with Mom, Dad, and kids at the top.

Our outlook could hardly be more horizontal than it is today. Indeed, that may be the essence of the matter—the right to get horizontal with anybody one chooses. The sexual impulse, a thing of awesome power, has at last overrun the fences and barricades erected by preceding generations for the defense of family and community well-being.

The evidences of such change are not just anecdotal but statistical. William J. Bennett's *Index of Leading Cultural Indicators* is particularly illuminating. We find, for instance, that divorces are 200 percent more numerous than they were thirty years ago. It is common among Americans forty-five years of age or older to observe that, when growing up, they knew no one who had been divorced. Today, half the people they or their children know seem to be in that state. For every unmarried female in 1960, there were 73.5 marriages and 9.2 divorces; the corresponding figures today are 55.7 and 21. That is change of amazing magnitude. Meanwhile, the percentage of children living with a divorced parent increased from 2.1 percent in 1960 to 9.5 percent by 1990. The percentage of children in single-parent homes— 90 percent of whom are fatherless—is three times as high as in 1960. To be born out of wedlock thirty years ago was to carry the stigma of the bastard—a stigma that no longer sticks, given that 28 percent of total births today are illegitimate.[1]

The placid acceptance of illegitimacy has been extraordinary. In 1960 only 2.3 percent of white births occurred out of wedlock. The figure for all races was a tiny 5.3 percent. Yet, behold what happened in just thirty years' time, as the sixties ethos permeated the culture: Illegitimacy increased by an astounding 400 percent! Twenty-one percent of white births in 1990 were to unwed mothers. And 65.2 percent of all black children born that year were illegitimate, compared to 23 percent in 1960.[2]

America in the nineties has "the highest teenage pregnancy rate of any country in the developed world." Early reversal of the trend seems unlikely. Sex, by all accounts, is among the most popular of all extracurricular activities. According to the Centers for Disease Control, in 1970 only 4.6 percent of fifteen-year-old girls had experienced sexual relations. By 1990 the figure was 25.6 percent. Among nineteen-year-olds, the figure was 75.3 percent, as opposed to 48.2 percent twenty years earlier.[3]

Another trend is that of educated and professional women bearing babies out of wedlock. The U.S. Census Bureau announced in 1993 that among never-married women ages eighteen to forty-four with children, 8.3 percent hold managerial or professional jobs, compared to 3.1 percent in 1982. More than twice as many such women (6.4 percent) hold bachelor's degrees as did a decade earlier.[4]

One could go on in this vein, but to no great purpose. What do the figures mean? They mean, in the most basic sense, that a new social ethic has acquired a large and growing measure of respectability. I did not say full respectability; the new ethic is likely not destined for majority status. And yet it has won a kind of toleration, a place at the national table of customs and mores, and not the meanest seat, either. The question is whether we should be glad or sorry.

The burden of proof is on the "glad" side. This is because never before has the ethos of full toleration for unwedded sex won anything approaching official acceptance. Society—meaning the visible consensus of clergy, teachers, authors, professional people, parents, public officials, and like leaders of thought—always has considered the public interest best served when sex and the breeding of children took place within matrimonial bonds.

There are persuasive reasons that may be easier to understand now than thirty years ago. In the old days, the defense of moral standards had a theoretical character: Such-and-such was the *right* thing to do, the only thing to do. It probably was, but the assertion generally had to be received in faith and trust. No longer is simple faith necessary for moral instruction. The liberated nineties have unmasked the unique perils of liberation. We find these perils are not theoretical in the least; they are real and tangible.

To desire sex outside of marriage today virtually assures having it. Where are the constraints after all? Sadly, large numbers of parents have been intimidated into silence. It has not been uncommon for two decades now to let an unmarried son and his visiting female friend share a bedroom (given that they're probably sharing one back at college). Is ministerial disapproval a constraint? Not with supernatural religion widely disbelieved or downplayed today, and with many ministers of the gospel falling in step with what they perceive as the spirit of the age. "The time has come," writes Episcopal Bishop John S. Spong, "for the church, if it wishes to have any credibility as a relevant institution, to look at the issues of single people, divorcing people, post-married people, and gay and lesbian people from a point of view removed from the patriarchal patterns of the past."[5]

Teachers are unlikely to endorse (much less to enforce) positions not in general favor at home or in church. The great majority of literary men and women—and their more influential counterparts on television—generally exhibit hostility toward moral norms. Thus extramarital sex loses the daring, avant-garde quality it enjoyed earlier in the century. (It becomes, one might almost say, disgustingly bourgeois!)

The drawbacks and disadvantages entailed by extramarital sex are not always easy to see. But they are of two kinds—personal and societal. Neither is independent of the other. We are not supposed to care greatly anymore what individuals do in private as long as it makes them happy. This stance—the essence of sixtiesism—has always struck the author as inherently selfish. One is not supposed to care about others? That is the inherent meaning of the claim that we are not to concern ourselves with others' free choices. But if a despondent individual's free choice is to hurl himself off the San Francisco Bay Bridge, only the most repugnant kind of noninterventionist would say to him, "Enjoy the dive." The infinitely more common (and natural) impulse is to grab the fellow by his coattail and hold on until help arrives. We are not quite the self-centered, "easy gratification" society we sometimes fancy ourselves to be.

Has this example any application in the moral realm? The author thinks it does; he believes it must. If a defective moral choice seems likely to ruin the chooser's life, it must be accounted the duty of society (or of society's members) to warn him, with zeal and fluency. Older, more traditional societies than ours sometimes restrained potential victims by force of law. We need not concern ourselves here with society's duty to wield human law in the defense of moral law. For one thing, we are a long way today from agreeing that a moral law even exists.

Let us consider simply the need to warn—and not solely for the potential victim's sake. Take the man on the bridge, for example. He may have a wife and small children, or these days a "significant other" (as the U.S. Census Bureau calls a sexual partner to whom one isn't married). His death could devastate his loved ones. He may have debts or obligations to others whose economic survival depends on his survival. Locked up in his skull may be the cure for cancer or AIDS. The point is the potentially *societal* character of this man's attempted deed. The ripples from his plunge into the bay would spread outward, dampening the futures of others.

Danger is easy enough to descry in the moral realm: It has an odor, an atmosphere, that mere statistics never can convey. What is the matter with sex outside of marriage? A vast number of things—things tangible and real, not born in the jealous minds of the sexually inhibited, but things alive in the universal human experience.

So, "sexual freedom," as it used to be called, has its joyous side; no one doubts this. But it has likewise its painful side. Marriage offers, for instance, the protection of contract. Such protection is wholly absent in the context of unwedded sex. Why does this matter? It matters because contract, civil or religious, expresses not just mutual rights but mutual obligations based on solemn promises. In the unwedded relationship, the emphasis is on rights—and this tends to get messy.

The whole basis of marriage is contractual, both in the moral and the legal sense. What most of us regard as the traditional marriage service comes from the Anglican *Book of Common Prayer* and before that from the formularies of the undivided church. The service is a web of mutual promises. The loving couple, hands joined, pledge "in the sight of God, and in the face of this company . . . to have and to hold from this day forward, for better for worse, for richer for poorer, in sickness and in health, to love and to cherish, till death us do part. . . ." A comprehensive set of pledges indeed! Is anything omitted? A chronically ailing child? Looming financial devastation? A change of heart or flagging interest? Nothing is omitted; all eventualities are included in the promise. Here is commitment in the fullest sense: It frees in the instant it binds. If the marriage vow forecloses quick escape from the relationship, so it affords freedom from gnawing anxiety, gained from the knowledge that one's partner is similarly bound. In such an environment mutual trust can grow: *We are in this together.*

Sex is among the marriage partnership's chief attributes and sources of strength. It becomes so by the exclusivity of the sexual relationship, the barring of outsiders from involvement at this exalted level. The circle cannot be opened to outsiders without damaging the whole environment of commitment.

It is almost ludicrously clear that in many modern marriages there is a gap between theory and practice. Not all marriages are lovingly committed; otherwise, why would there be a 50-percent divorce rate? Lawfully wedded husbands and wives sometimes beat each other up, ignore each other's basic needs, or abuse their own children, and sometimes all three. The point is not that not all marriages are good, because many are awful. The point is that the *institution* of marriage, based as it is on exalted promises, is good. Who is likely to honor a promise he has never made?

Defenders of unwedded sex do not necessarily disagree with such a premise. Some at least regard their own whispered promises to each other as elevated (if not superior). After all, such pledges are uncoerced by human ritual. But there is a transitory nature about most sexual relationships conducted outside of marriage. Some last a long time; the majority are brief—including some as brief as half an hour. Few such relationships embody much commitment. If the partners felt much commitment to each other, they would marry. The failure to do so puts their relationship at grave risk.

We do not need sociological studies to tell us this; we know it instinctively. The solemnity and grandeur of the marital promise brake the urge to renege. So much has been pledged! So many, with their own ears, have heard the pledges! Moreover, any relationship founded on contract places the contracting parties under mutual obligation. The contract can be dissolved only through painful and costly processes. Divorce is the formal renunciation of affection, the division of property and resources, the launching of a different kind of relationship with one's former spouse as well as one's children. The anguish inherent in the process is notorious and widely feared. At the same time, this fear may have positive effects. It may cause the squabbling partners to ask whether reconciliation does not make more sense than breakup.

None of these useful advantages obtains in unwedded relationships. A promise at the table or in bed—what is that against a solemn contract publicly declared? An argument over the dinner menu or where to sit in the theater has the potential to end abruptly an informal relationship. The man and woman have no mutually acknowledged incentive to resolve their differences of opinion (or, if they do, its power is less binding). Rather, in an environment where self-gratification often is the decisive factor, there can be every incentive *not* to resolve such differences.

But the nineties are impatient with arguments that because so-and-so is good for me, so-and-so is good for thee. Instead, we say, "Get your morality out of my face! What's it got to do with me?" Regarding unwedded sex, the question becomes: "Who cares? Is anyone really hurt by a one-night stand or a fling of a few months' duration?" The answer is yes. Nearly everyone involved in unwedded sex, directly or peripherally, gets hurt—one way or another.

We see this most clearly in understanding marriage as the relationship that confers the largest number of benefits on both partners. If marriage is the ideal for blending two lives, then any alternative to it represents a lower level of potential, attainment, and satisfaction. In turn, more unmarried relationships means fewer of the building-block institutions on which our society relies to rear children, transmit cultural values, and produce economic wealth and community health.

But it is more, and worse, than this. And now we must revisit current events. Among the principal purposes of sex is the procreation of children. It is so fundamental a purpose indeed that increasingly, as we have seen, the unmarried tend to procreate notwithstanding—obedient perhaps to an instinct more timeless and universal than has been supposed. So, in one sense, it has always been: passion outweighing prudence at levels high and low. Monarchs like England's King Charles II were particularly adept at, and singularly indifferent regarding the consequences of, royal reproduction. A point worth equal notice is that, unlike today, no one in good King Charles's time, least of all the king, trumpeted as a human right the propagation of illegitimate children.

Today the existence of this right, if so it may be called, is noised everywhere. It is in fact the stuff of show business, as Vice President Dan Quayle discovered unexpectedly, and to his sorrow, during the 1992 presidential campaign.

Quayle had thought only to reprimand Hollywood—at that, fairly gently—for extolling unwed motherhood; he discovered that many thousands of women believed themselves to have been insulted personally by his remark. These included not just unwed mothers like the fictional television personality Murphy Brown, but women who merely wanted to regard Murphy's example, should they aspire to it, as open and socially sanctioned.

Formal apologists for illegitimacy are numerous and articulate. Their paeans to single motherhood appear in national publications and on television. Increasingly one gets the idea that single motherhood is a new and exciting vocation. "We're living through the redefinition of the family," insists Leslie Wolfe, who heads Washington, D.C.'s Center for Women Policy Studies.[6] A research scientist in Dallas who the previous year had chosen to become an unwed mother considers the change inevitable. "In this day and age, you're kidding yourself if you think your marriage is going to last forever," she says. "Chances are, you're going to be a single parent anyway. This way, you don't have an ex-husband to deal with. I think it's really naive for women to think their husbands are going to be there forever."[7]

Who was the Vice President to be lecturing women of such enlarged social perspective? No public official seems likely in the near future to address this topic with anything approaching Dan Quayle's candor. In fact, the topic may fade entirely from political discourse. "A cat," said Mark Twain, "that has sat on a hot stove will not sit on one again; and he won't sit on a cold one either."

A distinctive trait these women share is affluence. Like Murphy Brown, the TV character, they tend to be well-educated and successful. The Dallas research scientist has (or had, at the time she was quoted) a nanny and a second home in New York City. Such women regard themselves as easily capable of making a go of unwed motherhood. In the economic sense, they are certainly right. If only this resolved the matter! But, of course, it does not—for two reasons.

First, the vast majority of unwed mothers are not affluent; they are poor. They have no nannies. Many might feel overwhelmed with joy at the prospect of working as a nanny. Barbara Dafoe Whitehead, in an Atlantic article entitled "Dan Quayle Was Right," says, "Children in single-parent families are six times as likely to be poor. They are also likely to stay poor longer. Twenty-two percent of children in one-parent families will experience poverty during childhood for seven years or more, as compared with only two percent of children in two-parent families."[8]

Whitehead's magisterial summing up of the case, not against but for Dan Quayle's Murphy Brown speech, was among the most important journalistic events of 1993. The evidence she marshaled in defense of intact, two-parent families amounted to cultural saturation-bombing. Down below, not a lot of intellectual infrastructure survived her concentrated assault.

Do we see what is going on here? Middle-class white women are busily propagandizing on behalf of a lifestyle— single motherhood—for which the hard evidence shows nonwhite, nonmiddle-class women to be hardly suited. The power of mass communications being what it is, much of this propaganda is bound to win acceptance. If those whose professional duty is telling America what to worry about are unworried themselves about illegitimacy, no alarm over illegitimacy will sound. Thus the trend can only be expected to deepen and broaden.

The poverty into which single-parent families sink is well-documented, but almost equally evident are the psychological effects on the children. Whitehead states: "Children in single-parent families are two to three times as likely as children in two-parent families to have emotional and behavioral problems. They are also more likely to drop out of high school, to get pregnant as teenagers, to abuse drugs, and to be in trouble with the law. Compared with children in intact families, children from disrupted families are at a much higher risk for physical or sexual abuse. . . . Children who grow up in single-parent or stepparent families are less successful as adults, particularly in the two domains of life—love and work—that are most essential to happiness."[9] Needless to say, not all such children belong to proudly unwed mothers. The majority of single-parent families began with two parents, only to fall apart under various pressures.

One would think that in any case the negative evidence regarding illegitimacy would discourage promotional campaigns by the determinedly unwed. Not so. *The New York Times* addresses the issue in a major feature story. The unwed mothers profiled are clamorously proud of themselves. But it appears not all is well: One woman's ten-year-old daughter begins to cry one night. "I don't know who my father is," she sobs. The mother tells her: "I feel bad, too. I wish we could have a dad who loves us both."[10]

"The father is a big issue," acknowledges Jane Mattes, founder of a national support group for unwed mothers, "and there are no books for this. You have to try to tell the child about the father as honestly as possible, but it may be years until they really get it."[11] One might think the collective experience of humanity to be of value, where it points to the pitfalls of illegitimacy. But, then, that might discourage new and old converts to the single-mother movement. The thing to do is simply to ignore or explain away the evidence.

The converts who speak publicly are relentlessly upbeat. In fact, it becomes clear on listening to them that these are not moral monsters but instead reasonably ordinary people, taking extraordinary steps in order to enjoy the once-ordinary satisfactions of family life. Anne Lamott, a novelist, tells readers of *The New York Times* why she became a single-mother-by-choice: She wanted a baby. And what a baby—Sam by name. "He is so beautiful that people stop us on the street. And he's turning out great—confident, smart, gentle, hilarious." She understands parenthood is no bed of roses. "You often have no idea what you're doing, and things keep going wrong, and your child is no help because he or she doesn't speak English yet. Every scrap of self-doubt gets magnified. You feel like a fraud."[12] But you love what you do.

And why is there no father standing elbow to elbow with her, gazing down into the crib? Because, although willing to have sexual relations with the man who became Sam's father, Anne Lamott lacked romantic feelings for him. "For instance, I did not sit around singing 'Let it please be him' whenever the phone rang. And we certainly did not expect to have a future together." Yet in a basic sense, they acted as though they did. Now he is gone. "I would give anything for Sam to have a great father," she tells friends, "because he wants one so badly, but I will not risk giving him a bad one."[13]

It is easy to like this woman. She appears to be that unfathomable, indispensable being, the natural mother, with a sense of humor thrown in for good measure. Yet she chooses to exercise this natural faculty outside the social-cultural-moral institution—the family—that is designed to meet the necessities of mothers.

This is an astounding departure. Not many years ago the strong likelihood would have been that Sam's father and Anne Lammott, novelist, on meeting, would have appraised each other as potential marriage partners: appraised, then come together or separated on the basis of that appraisal. Had they come together, in that grand structure of promise and obligation called matrimony, the most natural thing in the world would have been for them to participate jointly in the creation of life.

It is not so much that Anne Lamott's instincts have failed her as that the moral-cultural defenses to which she was entitled as a member of this society have been largely laid low. And we are only at the beginning of Sam's story: We know nothing yet of his future, except that a long journey awaits him. And we know, with Barbara Dafoe Whitehead, that the millions of children—legitimate or illegitimate—

who live in the increasing number of single-parent homes face formidable challenges. "Though far from perfect as a social institution," Whitehead writes, "the intact family offers children greater security and better outcomes than its fast-growing alternatives: single-parent and stepparent families. Not only does the intact family protect the child from poverty and economic insecurity; it also provides greater noneconomic investments of parental time, attention, and emotional support over the entire life course."[14]

The "moral revolution" of the past three decades—or, if you prefer, two centuries—has altered neither the fundamental conditions of human life nor the necessity of listening seriously to what a "traditional" moral perspective of life tells us about ourselves. Over against the possibly forced optimism of today's single-mother-by-choice stands the experience of the human race.

★ ★ ★

CHAPTER SIX

The Culture of Death

Every commentator on public matters acknowledges that there are matters on which the public simply will not come to a single mind. Argument in such cases is in vain. The parties merely restate familiar positions: *This* is so; *that* is so. Words and figures whiz past the disputants' heads without inflicting noticeable damage. One such issue is gun control—the right (constitutional) to bear arms versus the duty (imputed) to regulate the ownership and use of those arms. Of all irreconcilable differences to be found in the public square, the greatest separates the opponents and the proponents of abortion.

It is customary in politics to seek a middle ground on which the largest number of interested parties can stand comfortably. On abortion, there is no such middle ground, though this should hardly shock us. Abortion is only incidentally a political issue; it is most of all a moral issue, touching life itself—and whether life is worth protecting in all cases or only in some.

The issue arose in the 1970s as American society began reexamining the totality of its moral assumptions, the way a householder, moving to a new address, might sort through his possessions—holding on to the useful, discarding the unfashionable or worn-out. In the seventies—the backyard garden to the sixties and boasting many of the same exotic growths, only larger now—it seemed timely to scrutinize all moral strictures. Hadn't we taken aboard new, supposedly deeper understandings of human needs? Our ancestors' easy assumptions had worked well for them, but in this new age they had all the appeal of a stuffed moose head or a cardboard suitcase.

On these premises—the only ones that seemed to carry weight at that particular historical moment—the antiabortion laws were ripe for reappraisal. Abortion—that is, the entry of a doctor into the uterus to remove what might clinically be called the product of conception—was all about sex, but also about "rights." Sex and rights—two powerful human forces intersected explosively in the context of abortion. Up to this point the two had been strangers. Sex was as old as humanity; rights, in America, were at the roots of national origin. Yet sex had never been a matter of "rights." It had always been a matter of morals. And on the moral aspect of abortion, tradition spoke clearly enough. Abortion was wrong.

Granted, it had not been wrong in pagan times. The historian W. E. H. Lecky noted:

> The practice of abortion was one to which few persons in antiquity attached any deep feeling of condemnation. . . . The death of an unborn child does not appeal very powerfully to the feeling of compassion, and men who had not attained any strong sense of the sanctity of human life, who believed that they might regulate their conduct on these matters by utilitarian views, according to the general interest of the community, might very readily conclude that the prevention of birth was in many cases an act of mercy. . . .

No law in Greece, or in the Roman Republic, or during the greater part of the Empire, condemned it.[1]

The church changed all this. It took up with vigor the cause of the unborn, denouncing abortion (in Lecky's words) "not simply as inhuman, but as definitely murder. In the penitential discipline of the church, abortion was placed in the same category as infanticide."[2]

Why so? Because the church took a strictly nonutilitarian view of life. A life created by God was not to be judged by its usefulness to the community. Every life—a potentate's, a beggar's, a criminal's, an unborn baby's—had unique and innate worth. This is clearly something different from what we hear today. We hear that "unwanted" or severely handicapped children would be better off unborn.

The reason is that we have returned to the utilitarian conception of the Greeks and Romans. In that view, a life was measured by its value to the community—and often not even to the community but simply to the mother, in whom under our present dispensation resides the sovereign choice of giving birth or not giving birth. It is, in some sense, as though two thousand years had rolled away and the streets again were full of worshipers hastening up the hill to the columned temples of the gods. This sense of things becomes all the more vivid today as we see priests, ministers, and rabbis instructed by politicians to keep their "divisive" views to themselves and their flocks.

How did this shift take place? Some account of the process is necessary if only to show that the moral afflictions of the present day—drugs, crime, pornography—are all of a piece. In fact, they are members of a family—rather like the institution they labor to undermine. No genetic test is necessary to establish their kinship.

Simply put, sex and rights gave birth to the abortion controversy. It could not have happened otherwise. If a healthy and vigorous sex life is the great modern desideratum—the Holy Grail of a self-regarding society—that gives it special status in the community. Americans are used to respecting rights. The language of rights in our society has a venerable pedigree. "To secure" certain rights denied them, the colonists broke the "political bands" that connected them with the mother country. (A sort of political abortion in reverse?) The conception of rights in that time was highly limited by modern standards. The founding fathers were concerned with the rights that reinforced free government—speech, religion, trial by jury, etc. Sex did not function on the same level. One might say our ancestors failed to value sex enough. More likely, they just confined it to its historic context, which was moral and religious. Indeed, sex—as the early church had demonstrated in fighting abortion—was *too* important to be left to the politicians. Sex involved nothing less than the transference, from one party to another, of the supreme gift: life. Measured against this vital property, tariffs, roads, and standing armies were peripheral concerns.

There were no laws on abortion in early America. This in itself is an important point. It shows not government's indifference to questions of human life, but government's satisfaction that life was safe enough without the additional protections law could afford. Only later, in the nineteenth century, was the moral prohibition given the status of law, to combat a plague of determined abortionists selling their dangerous, unsanitary services.

This did not change much the way most Americans thought about abortion in the nineteenth and twentieth centuries. Churches continued to condemn the practice. The medical profession opposed abortion because it saw as its responsibility the preservation of life in every circumstance. The culture as a whole reinforced these views. Abortion was shameful, and the doctors who performed this "illegal operation" were "back-alley butchers." These were judgments not just on abortionists' professional techniques, but on their ethics. Did not the Hippocratic oath, which every neophyte doctor swore, forbid the administration of a "pessary" to effect spontaneous abortion?

Abortions occurred prior to the 1970s, as they had occurred for ages and would occur even if our government and culture suddenly united to restore the old status quo. Moral condemnation never results in the complete suppression of that which is condemned; it merely sets the cultural tenor. The point is not that abortions occurred even when the practice was outlawed; the point is that our culture, until quite recent times, took a far higher view of human life than is now the case.

Sex and rights—the older culture was not obliged to deal with this explosive combination. The sixties married, as it were, these sometimes competing concerns and brought them forcefully to public attention. It could be said actually that the sixties were about little else but sex and rights—specifically, how to get more of each. However, sex for sex's sake produced some disturbing aftereffects—namely, unwanted pregnancies. Many a sexually liberated woman of the sixties found herself unexpectedly expecting. The discovery that her ovaries had conspired with her partner's sperm to fulfill one of the grand human purposes might or might not have gladdened her heart. She might feel imposed upon: so much to do in life, so many exciting people with whom to do it. Now she would have to endure a nine-month pregnancy and a severe reduction in activities. She could lose her job. She had not reckoned on this. It was simply not fair!

So the question became: What to do next? The laws of forty-nine states flatly forbade abortion except to save the mother's life. Instead of advancing her quest for freedom, the state would retard it. And that seemed unfairest of all.

This became the vital observation: *the unfairness of her condition.* She had not meant to become pregnant; that was not at all her intention when she lay down with her lover. Perhaps she had employed "protection"; if so, it had failed her. Her attempts at self-realization and self-fulfillment had met with frustration. She was pregnant—her whole life had changed. But that of her male friend had not.

This last observation was all the more important during the sixties and seventies. The feminist movement, after some decades off duty, was reviving and stretching. Its tribunes nursed a certain resentment against men, who, while running society, managed to do pretty much what they wanted in life without facing similar setbacks or consequences. Why the disadvantages under which women labored—patriarchy, lower-paying jobs, the duty of bearing and raising children? The sixties offered a way out, through the assertion of rights. Courts and legislatures could do something about it. Accordingly, in the late sixties a powerful abortion-rights movement sprang up, clamoring for major reform of the abortion laws so that women wishing to end their pregnancies might do so, with no questions asked and no medical warnings or moral rebukes dealt out to the applicant. The rest is legal history.

The eventual assertion of a constitutional right to abortion necessitated some legal contortions worthy of Harry Houdini. No such right thitherto had been recognized as law. Throughout most of American constitutional history, the construction of rights had been narrow. Generally these had to do with citizenship: a right to vote, a right to the free exercise of religion, a right to own property, etc. Such rights underpinned the exercise of democratic responsibilities. The "right" to autonomy in one's bed—though it might sound quite reasonable—was a right largely unknown to legal precedent. The Constitution was not about two people giving each other love or pleasure; it was about government and citizenship and the protection of those civic virtues that kept us free.

However, judges are not vending machines, popping out a decision upon the insertion of an argument. Judges are flesh-and-blood people who spring from flesh-and-blood people. Whatever the people's preoccupations, they eventually win a sympathetic hearing from the people's magistrates. As sex—not citizenship—became our governing pre-occupation, it was natural that the courts became increasingly willing to search for ways of encouraging and supporting it. This is in fact what happened when the court decided *Roe v. Wade*. Whereas the court of Holmes and Taft or Frankfurter and Harlan would have laughed the abortion plaintiffs out of court, the justices in 1973 listened with interest and sympathy. In the end, the court found that, yes, there was a constitutional right to abortion—a right transcended by the antiabortion statutes of forty-six states.[3]

Again, horizontality had triumphed. A woman's body was her own, to do with as she liked; the Constitution guaranteed as much. So for this end the greatest minds and characters of the infant United States had labored through a steamy Philadelphia summer—to circumvent, constitutionally, a historic consequence of sex. The Supreme Court said that state legislatures could regulate some conditions for performing abortions; they could even ban all abortions in the final ninety days of pregnancy. But pregnant women gained from the justices the autonomy and power they had sought: No doctors, parents, clergymen, husbands, or lovers could ever again compel them against their will to become mothers.

It has worked out less splendidly than predicted. Simply put, the abortion rights movement has altered society's moral understanding. This has happened in various ways. One is the *narrowing and attenuating of sex;* not the broadening of sexual options, as widely advertised, but the reduction of sexual satisfactions. This is odd when you think of it. If sex and rights are what modern life is all about, then the right to sex on one's own terms should represent ultimate fulfillment. Oh, the endless, joyful nights—total choice, total abandonment! Or so the theory might run. But theory and reality on this occasion fail to coincide.

First, the severance of sex from its unique purpose—procreation—shrinks its domain, compressing the number and variety of occasions for giving and receiving joy. If sex is joy, the result should be joyful. But pregnancy, the most profound and certainly longest-lasting result of sex, revolts and repels large numbers of pregnant women—1.5 million of whom each year claim their constitutional privilege to (in the clinical phrase) "terminate their pregnancies." And what does this say about the *mutual* joy that should be found in sex? Pregnancy is by definition a joint act of creation. A man is involved. The child is half his, if such matters can truly be apportioned. The termination of a pregnancy, therefore, involves the rejection of his gift—that portion of him that fixed life in this impossibly tiny speck of plasm.

So much for mutuality. Sex on these terms becomes not a unifying act, but rather a divisive one. In this perspective, the man has done something to the woman which now the woman must remedy, at some pain and cost to herself. And the joy that any other couple might feel at this profound moment will not be shared by this pair. Both will be careful in the future to hold back and tighten up—to share not more but less.

In a novel both chilling and profound, *The Children of Men*, the British author P. D. James conjures up a time just around the corner when the human race is struck with universal sterility. How might this occur? "Pornography and sexual violence on film, on television, in books, in life, had increased and became more explicit," the narrator says, "but less and less in the West we made love and bred children. It seemed at the time a welcome development in a world grossly polluted by over-population. As a historian I see it as the beginning of the end."[4] Indeed, the more pseudo-pleasure, the less genuine pleasure; the more frantic the grappling, the less meaningful. So it goes in our time. The right to sexual freedom through abortion could not unreasonably be called antisexual.

A second way in which abortion has altered our moral perspective is by *decoupling religion from sexual biology*. The early church, as we have observed, taught the condemnation of abortion, a condemnation the religious community generally maintains today. Catholic priests, evangelical ministers, and laypeople in both church groups are at the forefront of efforts to restrict access to abortion or to halt it entirely and restore the old status quo. "In her vigorous concern for human rights and justice," Pope John Paul II said in Denver, Colorado, during his 1993 American visit, "the Catholic Church is unambiguously committed to protecting and cherishing every human life, including the life of the unborn."[5]

The clergy make no apology for this intervention in secular affairs, denying with some charitable exasperation that the matter is secular at all. They refuse to leave the matter to caucuses and back room maneuvering, or to earnest editorialists with master's degrees. Yet because they are clergy, the politicos and pundits would confine them to looking over the shoulders of those who wrestle with such matters. No moralizing and no finger-pointing, if you please! The priests, ministers, and rabbis reply that the politicians have it wrong; *they* are the poachers! Could the politicians please inform them where life originates? In the womb? Certainly. But who made the womb from whom the owner of the womb emerged? Is human life—that great wonder which grows more opaque the deeper we peer into it—a biological accident? If not, and if God is the author of creation, as our culture once affirmed universally, then God's wishes in the matter merit respect.

Here the politicians grow peevish. We are not gathered, they reply, to debate theology. The Constitution has placed theology on one side of public life and government on the other, and there they must remain in the interest of church-state separation. The church replies, "Hardly." The founding fathers, had they met to address matters of exclusive concern to the political order, would have found nothing to do. The earth is the Lord's, and the fullness thereof—or so the American people once believed, expressly or implicitly.

Still, it isn't clergy who control legislative and judicial posts, it is politicians. To these belong the last *official* word on the subject. They hold that the religious view of life—whether true or false, compelling or tedious—is not to be admitted into the discussion of abortion at the political or cultural level. To admit it would be to undermine the newly claimed right of abortion—and the secular intelligentsia certainly aren't willing to risk *that.* Many of its members see their "sexual freedom" waning in the event that the relationship between sex and religion is pinned down tightly. Yes, the religious may shout and heckle from the sidelines, as may all interested citizens—but only as long as they understand no one is obliged to pay them any heed.

This willful deafness to religious argument, so new in our history, has had various effects. A principal one is encouragement of the already widespread view that religion doesn't have a lot to do with modern concerns—the way people live, the way they think. If on the question of life's origins (as basic a question as can be imagined) religion is ruled out of bounds by secular referees, its claims to relevance in other matters, such as the integrity of the family, become harder than ever to substantiate. Religion becomes on these terms a harmless Sunday-morning pastime for people uninterested in the TV news panel shows.

In the abortion controversy secularist voices declare religion not just irrelevant but intrusive and overbearing, a threat to constitutional processes. This nuanced cry of alarm masquerades as concern for separation of church and state (a topic too broad for extended treatment in a book on morality). Suffice it to say that only in the past thirty years has America held excitably to the view that the preservation of our constitutional freedoms depends on snuffing out invocations at high-school commencements. Never in history has religion been so decisively shut out of an urgent dialogue as has been the case with abortion. If nothing else, this underscores the importance the present age attaches to abortion as both symbol and means of personal autonomy.

...And perhaps also of death wish? Malcolm Muggeridge has made that point, and it is well worth examining. The third way abortion has altered our moral perspective is through *undermining our natural respect for human life.* Every year in the United States more than 1.5 million abortions take place—a new Houston, Texas, foresworn and foregone in twelve months' time. Year after year the statistics beat against our sensibilities, becoming over time a part of the natural order, like typhoons in the Indian Ocean, like starvation in Africa. The difference is that every abortion results from a human decision. No such decision is natural to one who holds our society's former regard for human life. (Not just unborn life, but life itself as the gift of that same God who in the nineties is in such bad odor with our intellectual leaders.)

Social commentators sometimes write of the "slippery slope," the dizzying descent from order to chaos and sanity to madness commencing with a single false step, usually of a public-policy nature. Abortion clearly is "Point A" on such a slope, at whose bottom lies broad indifference to human life and suffering. It would seem a vast transformation indeed for a sentimental people like the Americans to give over all traces of human sympathy; even today we turn out in droves to search for missing children, contribute billions to charity, and offer services to volunteer activities of genuine benevolence. Yet in the age of abortion it is not only the unborn who are at risk, but also the elderly and "used up." A spreading euthanasia ("good death") movement is taking hold, with the idea of giving the hopelessly ill the legal right to kill themselves or else have a doctor do it. Though "right-to-die" enthusiasts might phrase it less callously, there is some sentiment to the effect that the very sick are better off dead—a quick *coup de grace* preferable to painful, lingering existence. Such are the sentiments of Dr. Jack Kevorkian's "patients." These sufferers have put themselves in the hands of the celebrated "suicide doctor" who can assist them in killing themselves (gently, or course).

The distinction between "self-deliverance," as suicide exponents sometimes call these acts, and outright mercy killing is exceedingly fine. Perhaps in the former case, the victim genuinely wishes to die; perhaps in the latter case, another—a man or woman of impeccable professional skills—calls the turn. But in a broad sense, it probably doesn't matter: Once you've established the principle that the unfit, the inconvenient, and the burdensome have fewer rights than the rest of us, the point becomes moot. Has not abortion entrenched that principle fairly solidly? The mother decides on behalf of her unborn infant what kind of life the two of them might lead should the birth take place. That seems fine, because the child, the objection arises, is only partially formed in the womb. Yet is it much different with the adult who, by reason of his debility, is partly *unformed*? What about AIDS sufferers, cancer victims? Could not a society concerned about medical costs argue that such as these are not worth what they cost to treat and keep alive? After all, we have heard a former state governor declaim on the duty of terminally ill people "to die and get out of the way, with all our machines and artificial hearts and everything."[6]

Among the most compelling (or arresting, if you will) reasons offered for abortion twenty years ago concerned the likelihood of a child's being born with a defect sure to mar or shorten his life. As a newspaper reporter, the author helped cover the first hearings in Texas on legislation intended to liberalize the state's stringent abortion law (the one subsequently invalidated in *Roe v. Wade*). These hearings presented to the legislative gaze photographs of deformed babies. Hearts were openly touched, though the legislature at that point declined to alter the law. In more recent times doctors have refused on like grounds to ensure the survival of children born with afflictions such as Down's syndrome. These children die—but the principle on which one would stand, shrieking in protest against such cruelty, is more elusive than it was twenty years ago.

The grounds for moral judgment contract where permission is granted the individual to take, extinguish, foreclose (insert your favorite word) that human life our ancestors understood to be the gift of God. Today, with feet on the slippery slope, downward we coast. The ride can be exhilarating. The finish, in its own way, is certain to be memorable.

CHAPTER SEVEN

Pornography

In the early sixties, at a formerly grand theater gone to seed, the author saw—shhhhhh!—his first, and practically last, pornographic movie. It was pornographic, mind you, by the standards of that comparatively pale and innocent time. By the standards of the nineties the film would have to be judged naive and bumbling. A few women of varying charms gamboled seminude—and that was the extent of the stimulation. There were no scenes of lovemaking, much less copulation. There was no mutilation, no sadomasochism. The plot was based on, of all things, a Rudyard Kipling poem, "The Women." Literature and lechery in the same offering. What more could wide-eyed college students desire?

Pornography in the Kennedy years was not yet the skull-and-crossbones of cultural revolt, a raspberry in the face of decorous taste. It was very much what it had been for centuries—bawdy, boisterous, leering, slyly winking, altogether a matter of personal preference, and most of all, in its relation to the larger culture, reserved.

The transformation of pornography from a modest underground industry to a force for cultural change is among the signal events of the past thirty years—an extraordinarily short time for such a transformation. Yet this change hardly has occurred in a vacuum. The best way to understand it is as one snorting, panting part of the late-twentieth century's revolt against traditional morality.

The modern pornography industry and its slime-encrusted works, for all the anger and opposition they rightly excite, are as much a symptom as a cause of the present depression in moral understanding. Yet, deeply embedded by now in the fiber of the culture, it plays a larger and larger role in deadening our reaction to the behavior it exalts. Movies, television, commercial advertising, and music combine to beam a message of raw desire and the need to satisfy it promptly. And the more this message is broadcast, the more normal it seems. Pornography is no longer a matter of little old men reaching beneath the counter to produce with a wink and a flourish a cheap publication guaranteed to excite. We are far beyond the famous "feelthy postcards" of yore. The signal fact is that comparatively little these days is adjudged "feelthy" by either the industry that produces it for sale or the legal authorities who monitor its content. Society collectively has pushed the limits of acceptability far beyond what could have been foretold or even imagined twenty or thirty years ago. No part of the human anatomy is exempt from depiction in magazines or videos that enjoy wide distribution, nor is any human sexual activity out of bounds—bestiality, mutilation, bondage, torture, even reportedly sex-cum-murder. The immediate point is that we have descended so because we have wanted to, not because anybody has made us do it.

This is a point not easily grasped, so familiar are the condemnations of pornography heard across the political spectrum, from feminists on the left to pro-family activists on the right. As a journalist, the author has participated in those condemnations. (He also is all for locking up a broad assortment of pornographers, as in the good old days when human beings regarded the human body as a thing possessed of dignity. However, the modern tendency to confuse pornography with constitutionally protected "speech" normally nullifies attempts to deal severely with sleaze artists.) The fact remains that pornography would not exist but for the laws of economics. These stipulate that whatever is demanded by a party offering to hand over money, that product shall be made available by a second party. This is not to blame or condemn the marketplace; proximate blame lies with the people for desiring and demanding what they and others before them once considered degrading.

We return once again to this book's thesis and its definition: morality as a series of propositions about human nature—who we are, what we're doing here, what best fulfills our nature. What do we believe is best? Family relationships based on love between man and woman? If so, that is what we will read about. It is what our movies and our love songs will be about. "You are the promised kiss of springtime," we will sing, "that makes the lonely winter seem long."[1]

But perhaps a different view is taking root—a view of man and woman as disconnected individuals living on terms of easy freedom, seeking pleasure where it may be found and taking that pleasure without concern for its consequences (far less its imputed obligations). This will occasion new songs, new lyrics. We have now 2 Live Crew and the delicate ditty, "Me So Horny." We will have, on a broader scale, the culture of the nineties, a culture we have made with our own hands and hearts.

The culture of the early, as distinct from the later, sixties did not condone pornography any more than it condoned abortion, family breakup, divorce, disorder in the classroom, and a long list of modern tribulations with a common core (a core of self-regard above all else). Decades of egalitarianism have brought us finally to this point. Everything is equal; every*one* is equal. Verticality is dead; the horizontal is king.

A culture of respect creates for pornography only enough room to protect what might be construed as the manufacturers' rights to free speech. For the rest, the culture states its high regard for human beings and hopes that good opinion takes hold generally. After all, there is not much peace if citizens go around demonstrating their low regard for fellow citizens.

In particular our culture historically has demonstrated its regard for women. Why women? Because men were stronger and coarser by nature and, therefore, were supposed to smooth down their jagged edges as homage to the women whose more domestic virtues made civilization possible. The rule of thumb was "Ladies first," or, at sea, "Women and children first in the lifeboats" (the so-called Birkenhead Rule, named for the British vessel whose crew and passengers originated it). Men were not to swear in front of women, and, if they slipped and did so, were to offer fervent apologies. When a man met a woman on the street, off came his hat; bareheaded he stood until the two parted company.

All of this has a precious, archaic quality to it, though such standards were in general effect little more than thirty years ago. Could Americans really have taken so nonegalitarian a view of the relationship between the sexes? The triumphs of the feminist movement have made us partially forget how radical the changes really have been. Down from what remained of her pedestal (which feminists had been chipping to pieces since the twenties) stepped the Liberated American Woman, into an age in which deference no longer was automatic.

The women's rights movement did not of itself nudge the pornography industry onto the road to riches. But the equalizing of women and men was a factor in the industry's booming growth. The sixties brought death to distinctions of any sort, and the egalitarian society that took root in that feverish time preached only one kind of preference—the new over the old, the instinctive over the "artificial." Whatever men and women had valued in the past was, by the values of the sixties, elitist, repressive, even fascist. All were equal now. All were to "do it" without looking back, counting the cost, or calculating the likely results.

An age with this ethos cannot be greatly surprised when instincts of all sorts rise to the surface. Where were the restraints of old? Gone, completely. Absent any kind of social consensus, there can be no guidelines (and no safety). And absent guidelines, there can be no consensus. So it came to pass in the late sixties that the loudest, most insistent voices in the culture declared sexual liberation valuable and vital. This meant that so grand a cause had no visible limits. What is one to say—this much liberation and no more? Of course not. Liberation ends when nothing remains worth liberating, at least in the liberators' judgment.

Regarding pornography, only a few pre-sixties scruples remain. Not quite everything goes, though infinitely more goes than was the case thirty years ago. Child pornography, which is produced on a mass scale and widely retailed, remains not only illegal but taboo even among people of spacious liberal convictions. Indeed, the innocence of children is a concept of which the liberated nineties has not let go. More curious to see is the intense opposition that pornography meets among some feminists, many of whom act in open alliance with the otherwise abhorred "religious right." This is curious because most often feminists favor the expansion of personal choice; and a taste for pornography might count as the kind of responsible choice we are supposed to favor. However, feminists argue, with some pith and potency, that pornography degrades and debases women, causing them harm.

Recently Canada's Supreme Court agreed unanimously that "materials portraying women as a class as objects for sexual exploitation and abuse have a negative impact on the individual's sense of self-worth and acceptance."[2] Similarly, a U.S. federal circuit court declared in 1985 (in spite of striking down the antipornography ordinance in question) that "depictions of subordination tend to perpetuate subordination. The subordinate status of women, in turn, leads to affront and lower pay at work, insult and injury at home, battery and rape on the streets."[3] The federal pornography commission that reported to the Reagan Administration in 1986 reached similar conclusions.

These judgments may sound subjective, but the odd truth is, they embody the old wisdom kicked out the door by the liberated sixties—now being picked up from the streets and carried cautiously back into the temples of justice. Repeated depictions of the once-shocking as ordinary and even fun give such things the appearance of everydayness. Such an appearance diminishes the inhibitions (and moral instincts?) with which members of the modern culture might still be saddled. What the judges and feminist lawyers are saying, in essence, is that we may have lost our capacity for shock. This in itself amounts to a very unsixties-like admission—that some things are innately shocking. We have not done away with verticality after all, it seems. There remains, for limited purposes at least, a hierarchy of values: this species of conduct preferable to that one.

Much more than matters of taste are involved here. The U.S. Circuit Court claims that the perception of women as subordinate leads to injury and even rape. There is at the very least documented evidence that many rapists and murderers use pornography. Dr. James Dobson, founder and president of Focus on the Family, a national organization working to reinvigorate traditional family values, quotes a letter he received from the serial killer Ted Bundy declaring that "pornography is a force that plays a vital role in violent behavior." Bundy, who was soon afterward executed by the state of Florida, confessed that he himself had been a pornography devotee. However, he added: "I am *not* saying pornography *caused* me to do certain things. I am not blaming it. It is far more complex than that."

The whole phenomenon of pornography is complex. It excites and it depresses. It depicts the complete human form, and yet it reduces the owner to simian status, a "trousered ape" in C. S. Lewis's phrase (assuming the trousers are actually in place). Pornography's low, cynical view of human nature is consistent with the other paramount signs of our times—broken families, broken lives, broken hearts.

The old pornography had its cheerful side; the new is cheerless in the extreme, grimly convinced that humans are, after all, a sorry lot.

What is still more troubling is that judging by their consumption of this material, many humans agree with that view, or at least are seriously tempted by it. The creators and suppliers of pornography, unsavory crew as they may be, are entrepreneurs, offering a product no denizen of the nineties is compelled to purchase (and from which one would recoil if he or she entertained a more exalted vision of human nature). Who are we? What best suits our nature? Pornography conceals the answer, with our own complicity.

CHAPTER EIGHT

"Straight" Talk on Homosexuality

There are no new moral perplexities. Only the guises in which they appear are new and not always even then.

We know, for instance, that homosexuality has been practiced from that time "whereof," in Blackstone's phrase, "the memory of man runneth not to the contrary." W. E. H. Lecky, with Victorian delicacy, omitted mention of it from his long, learned disquisition on European morals. Yet homosexuality was open and visible in ancient civilizations like Greece, where, as Crane Brinton relates, an older warrior and a younger "were assumed to play psychologically a masculine, and, therefore, noble, role, the older man essentially teaching the younger, preparing him for his future part in this world of heroes, fighters, competitors, *men*, still in so many ways of the spirit of the world of Homer."[1]

The account in Genesis of Sodom and Gomorrah is famous for the passage in which the men of Sodom clamor for Lot to bring out the two angels in human form he was sheltering so that they could have sexual relations with them. From Sodom comes the term *sodomy,* which, according to Webster's Second International Dictionary, means "carnal copulation in any of certain unnatural ways."

The description is uncomplimentary. As are the vast majority of judgments rendered on homosexuality throughout history—the Greeks notwithstanding. Most often homosexuality's lot has been general condemnation. We must ask why this is so, but first we have to notice that no such question reared its head thirty years ago—not within general hearing, anyway. Maybe the topic arose in college sociology seminars, in the coffeehouses of the day, or in little-read publications of an intellectual bent; but rarely elsewhere. The common assumption then regarding "same-sex relations," to cite the modern euphemism, was that one shouldn't engage in such relations, and if one did, well, nothing good would come of it. The supposition seemed not so much acquired as innate. The superiority of the heterosexual relationship was one of those things that Americans, as the political philosopher Willmoore Kendall put it, knew "in their hips."

But heterosexual Americans are much less confident today concerning this assumption—not because their convictions have changed but rather because of what they can say publicly without inviting explosive retaliation. The large and highly articulate gay rights movement regards all criticism of the homosexual lifestyle as a personal assault on homosexuals. The response is to assault critics with cries of "homophobia" (literally, fear of homosexuals) and "gay-bashing" (the verbal mugging of homosexuals). Not all the critics mind the countercriticism, but others are intimidated into silence. Gay rights spokesmen, one quickly learns from encounters with them, are always right and their critics always wrong. Anything short of all-out devotion to their program counts as gay-bashing. The movement's overall aim is to acquire society's consent to the proposition that homosexuality is as attractive and valid a "lifestyle" as heterosexuality. This consent, should it be gained, would represent the most revolutionary change in the history of Western morals. All of our understanding about sex and sexual relations would be turned upside down. Gay rights leaders suggest this is why heterosexuals oppose the movement so strenuously: They are afraid of dispossession and jealous of the special status heterosexual society has always accorded them. The truth is otherwise.

Why has homosexuality suffered condemnation throughout history? What is the problem, exactly? We ransack the historical record, and when all is said and done, we find that among the varied groups that have encountered over the centuries social opposition and distaste, homosexuals are singular. The disapproval they protest against has been ubiquitous and consistent. Even Jews, the most persecuted and victimized religious minority, could not claim (even if they wanted to) anything like the long record of opposition to which professed homosexuals have been exposed. Here and there, from time to time, Jews and Christians would reach informal understandings that allowed the two religions sprung from ancient Judaism to live with minimal friction. Homosexuals, by contrast, can point to no extensive accommodation they have received. There may have been some enclaves of marked tolerance, such as in the theater or in British public schools in the late nineteenth and early twentieth centuries. There is little other evidence of tolerance, much less accommodation. The failure of one group ever, anywhere, to win substantial accommodation from the larger society raises serious questions about the behavior the group would like to have accommodated. It raises the question: Does that behavior accord with the strongest, most thoroughly informed views of what is natural—i.e., true to nature—and what is not?

The traditional view of sex is of a physical relationship between a man and a woman. That relationship—heterosexuality—is anchored in infinitely more than theory and teaching. Biology accords it the most sweeping kind of endorsement; the male and female sexual organs accommodate each other exactly. And the biological argument continues from there: Male-female coupling, as everyone knows, produces babies, and babies replenish the human species. This kind of elementary evidence would seem to render heterosexual relations completely natural, agreeable with the order of things.

However, this does not quite answer the question Is homosexuality, as Webster's definition suggests, *un*natural? What if not one but two kinds of sexual expression are agreeable with nature? The easy and straightforward answer is that natural laws are restrictive. Water flows downhill. Trees grow upward. Water is wet. Fires burn. But two kinds of sex, side by side? At minimum, the assertion is peculiar.

There are certainly two kinds of gratification that sex affords. One is procreative. In terms of this function, we must note the barrenness of homosexuality. By definition, a homosexual relationship is one of childlessness (a disability that certain homosexuals are beginning to challenge by adopting children).

The other kind of gratification, of course, is the pleasure of physical contact—sometimes soft, sometimes fiery, but above all shared. Homosexuality makes explicit claims on this ground; that two men or two women are lovers rather than a man and a woman supposedly is irrelevant. It is the sharing of physical love that is said to matter most. But the homosexual act is actually a parody of the heterosexual, which it imitates without the full means of imitation. The rectum—an organ designed for the disposal of bodily waste—is a strange and inferior substitute for the female vagina, one of whose chief functions is to receive the male sexual organ. The most anyone could reasonably say about the "naturalness" of homosexuality is that the desire behind it—the desire for sexual gratification—is natural. However, the means of expression is not natural (unless the meaning of "nature" is other than we have believed it to be for thousands of years). The fuller expression—indeed the *only* full expression—of sexual love is the male-female relationship.

Natural versus unnatural: What has any of this to do with the topic of morality? The simple answer is that we are examining the roots of our moral crisis. We must ask, accordingly, How does "gay rights" bear on that condition? What must we make of this movement specifically, and how ought our society to regard the practitioners of homosexuality in general? Such questions, while virtually unimaginable thirty years ago, are of urgent importance today. The mission of the gay-rights movement is nothing less than the reordering of sexual norms to accommodate homosexual desires and tastes. This is a momentous business to say the least. We can only guess at the potential consequences. The movement, having appropriated for its own purposes the ancient word *gay* (meaning "lively" or "spirited"), has issued a strenuous challenge to the word's former owners, the "straights." The challenge is to accord homosexuals and their "lifestyle" complete, unstinting equality with heterosexuals and the heterosexual "lifestyle."

This is an exquisitely "nineties thing" to request. The moral crisis, we will recall, revolves around the frenetic quest for equality, in moral norms as well as in access to the voting booth. Like the abortion rights movement, gay rights has adopted the language not of moral or theological discourse but of the civil-rights crusade. Its language is the language of law. Morality, to the gay-rights movement, is a secondary issue; moralists judge other people's private behavior, and the Constitution acknowledges no such right. The only applicable right, in fact, is the right to do whatever one wants without hurting someone else.

The stratagem must be called inspired. An age besotted on "equality" can respond only with interest and often sympathy to the claims of a supposedly disenfranchised group, particularly one that portrays itself as the target of hateful words and deeds. Gay-rights activists like to compare themselves to the civil-rights leaders whose actions and tactics helped pull down the formidable edifice of racial segregation in post-World War II America. When in 1993 President Clinton proposed to open military service fully to homosexuals and lesbians, backers of the measure compared it to President Truman's executive order racially integrating the military in 1947. Justice was what homosexuals were after—simple justice. Someday they would overcome. One would never imagine, on hearing such rhetoric, that the activities in dispute were other than natural and logical.

Lawsuits, a favorite tactic of civil rights proponents, are popular among gay-rights activists as well. A favorite target of these suits is state laws that ban and penalize sodomy. The U.S. Supreme Court set back this strategy by upholding Georgia's right to pass and enforce a sodomy law (*Hardwick v. Bowers*). The court said there existed no "fundamental right to engage in homosexual sodomy." However, there are always legislative ears to be whispered into, legislative arms to be bent back. The gay-rights movement's success in the legislative sphere has been impressive. Numerous cities have enacted ordinances that protect gay rights. St. Louis's, passed in late 1992, is stronger than many others but not atypical: It bars discrimination in housing, credit, employment, education, and public access, all on various grounds. The most conspicuous of these grounds is sexual orientation. Violators are to pay fines of up to $500 and go to jail for up to ninety days. (At the time about 130 cities had similar laws.)

Another tactic of the movement is to campaign for laws and ordinances recognizing the sexual partners—male or female—of government workers to be full-fledged dependents, eligible for health insurance and other benefits. This means that homosexual "partners" are entitled to dependent status as wives and husbands.

There has been a predictable backlash to such enterprises: Instead of extending legal protection to gays, several communities have voted to repeal or bar the passage of laws that create special rights for particular classes of citizens.

Among those special rights is the claim to exemption from the consequences, if any, of pursuing a homosexual lifestyle.

The divisive nature of the gay-rights campaign is obvious at once. It asks that Americans suddenly drape a protective arm around the shoulders of citizens whose distinguishing characteristic—for purposes of the request, at least—is a sexual proclivity at odds with traditional moral understanding. In short, after centuries of acquaintance with the moral law and its stipulations, Americans are told to forget it. There is a new plan, a new program—the old one is off. Various members of the intelligentsia, whether homosexual or not, have been happy to chime in with messages of support. Episcopal Bishop John Shelby Spong contends that homosexuality and heterosexuality are equivalent orientations, "neither good nor evil. . . . Both aspects of sexuality will ultimately be seen as natural. . . . Our pious conditional resolutions binding moral homosexuality to celibacy reveal nothing less than an irrational belief in a sadistic God, in the light of new knowledge."[2]

This "new knowledge" is widely advertised. Certainly Spong himself makes much of it. The idea is that homosexuality cannot be considered a conscious choice—it is, rather, an orientation, the product of internal forces such as give one man a taste for jazz, another a flair for polo.

We would not wish to punish or disadvantage a citizen for what he cannot help, would we? Gay-rights leaders understand thoroughly the nature of the tactical advantage they are trying to seize. Whereas they spoke formerly of "sexual preference," the term today is "sexual orientation"—an easier pill for the general public to swallow, they hope, than unnatural sex by personal and individual choice. Every new scientific study that might suggest as much is leaped upon. According to Spong (who makes pronouncements on biology as confidently as on theology), in homosexuals a prenatal "sexing" of the brain takes place where sexual desire is born. One subsequent study pointed to a "gay gene" that *may* determine sexual orientation. Among recent submissions is a study by the National Cancer Institute that suggests "a genetic link to homosexuality."[3]

It is unnecessary in the short compass of this book on morality to take a lingering look at biology. It may suffice to say that none of these studies goes farther than merely to *suggest* a genetic link to homosexuality. National Cancer Institute researchers acknowledge that if a gene influences homosexuality, that gene "has not yet been isolated."[4] The retired Harvard biologist Ruth Hubbard, writing in *The New York Times*, notes the "near impossibility of establishing links between genes and behavior."[5] It is all speculation, guesswork, made riskier (if showier) by the political character of the guesswork. Gay rights has turned gays, who are large political contributors, into a constituency that cannot be omitted from any large political calculation, least of all in states where they are numerous, like California and New York.

Beyond this, the gay-gene studies sound an odd note—a defensive, deterministic one. If homosexuality is, after all, so joyous and enriching a lifestyle, why the quest to prove it involuntary? Wouldn't it make more sense to advertise it as an option any and all might follow with profit? Why not meet the "straight" society head-on and convince it that homosexuality is as noble and as bracing as vintage bordeaux? No doubt the failure to do so bears some relationship to the sparseness of the evidence that might support such a claim.

Yet the public pretense is that homosexuals are different only in bed. "We are your sons and brothers (or daughters and sisters)" is a slogan that appears frequently on gay-rights placards. The idea is that we know you, and you know us; and this permits homosexual activists to agitate for more than tolerance—that is, for a social seal of approval.

There are various things wrong with tolerance, from the homosexual standpoint. For one thing, tolerance has to be conferred—as King Henry IV, with royal condescension, extended tolerance to France's minority Protestants in 1598 via the Edict of Nantes. As for the tolerated, they tend to feel like fifth wheels—permitted to function, but always with other people's eyes on the backs of their necks. They remain outsiders to the community consensus. This does not feed their self-esteem, which for people living in the 1990s seems to be a central element of the human makeup, and virtually a right. Most disagreeable of all, tolerance can be suddenly and savagely withdrawn. The French Protestants offer an example. Louis XIV, with catastrophic effect, revoked the Edict of Nantes. For the Catholics, it was back to persecuting Protestants.

For various reasons, then, homosexual activists crave more than tolerance—they want legitimation. If homosexuality is as good as heterosexuality, only different, then every right the larger society has to offer is theirs, with no quibbling. Whatever they wish to do, they may do, without fear of retribution or violence. One wonders how sincerely gay activists believe in the possibility of the full acceptance of a "lifestyle" that society historically has not admired, to say the least. It may be that activists have adopted this strategy in the spirit of those politicians who ask for twice as much as they really want or expect, and count it a victory when they get only half.

Certainly gay rights activists have been vocal—and effective. Their pressure persuaded trustees of the American Psychiatric Association in 1973 to change their minds about homosexuality as a mental disorder. Activists had disrupted two of the group's national meetings, demanding that learned doctors stop calling them sick. Sympathetic psychiatrists began to toil from within the system, and, lo, the trustees, in a decision later ratified by the whole membership, voted to strike homosexuality from the official manual of psychiatric disorders. The trustees also deplored discrimination against homosexuals in areas such as employment and housing.

Gay groups clamor for educational materials that represent homosexuality with sympathy, as, for instance, the briefly celebrated children's book *Heather Has Two Mommies*. Authorized for use in New York City schools, the book related that although Heather's mommy had a lesbian lover, this really was nothing novel or alarming, and Heather should be glad for the extra attention this state of affairs made possible. The New York City school superintendent's attempts to impose the book on communities made up of more "old-fashioned" families aroused so much anger locally that the superintendent lost his job (but only after ousting the "old-fashioned" members of a school board in Queens and appointing his own). In Texas, homosexual advocates have demanded textbook treatment of homosexuality and bisexuality in cases when "a man's love or passionate affection for another man, or a woman's love and commitment to another woman, are crucial to their work and actions."[6]

Gay journalists—who have their own national organization—have been successful at persuading mainstream publications to hire them specifically as reporters and commentators on the lifestyle they practice. This is odd indeed. There are no reporters conveying news of the heterosexual community. (Gays might rejoin that nearly all news, by implication at least, shows forth heterosexuality. What about all those wedding write-ups?) In fact, the success of straights at monopolizing the marriage scene angers many gay activists, who in turn clamor for full legal recognition of gay "unions" (the operative term for now at least). Some liberal clergymen, engaging in theological improvisation, have extended homosexuals this very right. Yet the nation briefly underwent convulsions after President Clinton announced his plan to open military service to practicing homosexuals. Partly because the military objected strongly, the president fell far short of his goal. But his original proposition may rise again one of these days.

For all of these efforts, the singularity of the homosexual lifestyle continues to stand out. Recent studies contradict gay-rights claims that 10 percent of Americans are gay. The latter claim derives from Alfred Kinsey, founder of the celebrated sex-research institute bearing his name, who adduced the figures in 1948. (His precise claim was that 10 percent of males over sixteen years of age practice homosexuality exclusively for periods of up to three years. Kinsey was notoriously unselective in choosing his interview subjects: Around a fourth of males he spoke with were, or at one time had been, prisoners; many interviewees attended his sex lectures; and two hundred were male prostitutes. A fine cross section of 1940s America!) Though the 10 percent figure is a longtime staple of gay-rights rhetoric, other studies fail to confirm it. In fact, studies in this country and elsewhere point to homosexual populations, temporary or exclusive, as low as 0.7 percent (France), 1.4 percent (Britain), and 1.2 percent (the United States).[7]

Yet even if 99 percent of the population were homosexual and just 1 percent were heterosexual, the question still would be: Which practice agrees with human nature? Both, or just one? Transitory majorities are not sovereign in moral matters. A majority that lacks bolstering evidence for its claim is no more than a snapshot of brief consensus that may rapidly fade.

The author cannot pretend that gay-rights groups will accept his characterization of the sexual practices they have made their own; such groups have their own characterizations. The author further notes even so that "his" characterization is not really his—it is the human race's, proceeding from thousands of years of experience and observation. Gay-rights groups reply that the traditional construction of their ways and means is informed by bigotry and hatred. Not necessarily.

As we saw earlier, we need not lean very hard on the anatomical evidence; it is obvious. Still, it does not resolve the question: What of different strokes for different folks, as a post-sixties saying had it? Fly rods vs. cane poles, Toyotas vs. Hondas—is this not the kind of preference we talk of with respect to homosexuality? Not at all. Fishing equipment and automobile preferences have few, if any, notable consequences. A sexual preference, almost by definition, is freighted with consequences.

The family, for example, is founded on the heterosexual relationship. No man-woman sex, no families—the matter is as clear as that. Once it would have seemed extraneous, if not downright silly, to expend effort proving the worth of the family. That worth we knew in our hips. (Not the oddest feature of civilization in the nineties is the necessity of explaining even the obvious.) The command to be fruitful and replenish the earth is received on the highest authority, but even a determined secularist will acknowledge that, absent fruitfulness, the human species disappears.

The likelihood that the gay-rights movement, however articulate and well-organized, could ever overthrow the heterosexual family must be counted marginal. That is not to say that the movement, given present objectives, is incapable of inflicting harm on perceptions of family life and on family structure. In fact, the clamor for legitimation of homosexuality is deeply harmful to families. It confuses the purposes for which families are formed. Granted, few in the larger society care deeply whether homosexuals or lesbians pair off (in sad parody of the marriage relationship) and reside together. When homosexuals court visibility, however, and seek cultural and legal sanction for their relationship, it becomes society's affair.

The family is more than a reproductive device; it is a training ground. As Rita Kramer writes, "The traditional nuclear family as we have defined it remains the chief agency—and the best one—for developing character in the individual and for transmitting the values of the culture. . . . We are all influenced by our environment, by the society we live in, but the most pervasive environment remains the family that shapes us, and the most effective form of social action is still arguably the bringing up of children with a sense of self and feeling for others, with goals that give meaning to their lives."[8] The National Commission on Children, chaired by U.S. Senator John D. Rockefeller IV and comprising liberals and conservatives alike (including then-Governor Bill Clinton of Arkansas), declared its "collective view that families and the circumstances of their lives will remain the most critical factor affecting how children develop and fare."[9]

What, then, shall our families teach—that heterosexuality, on which the family is founded, is equivalent to homosexuality, which denies the sexual basis of the family? Gay-rights activists would clearly have it so. But we must consider where this sort of thinking leads. If heterosexuality is no more than a lifestyle option, then there is no social need to prefer it. Parents accordingly should let children discover and pursue their "sexual orientation." Nor is there reason, in such a case, not to recognize legally any personal relationship that the persons involved might choose to declare. As we have noted, numerous levels of government have acknowledged this supposed obligation, extending legal rights to domestic "partners" of the same sex and protecting gays by statute.

Such moves have strikingly personal effects. In Madison, Wisconsin, for instance, in the early nineties, two heterosexual women attempted to oust a lesbian roommate from their apartment. The lesbian filed a grievance with the local human rights board and won $1,500 in damages from her "homophobic" ex-roommates, who additionally had to send her a public letter of apology and undergo sensitivity training on homosexuality.

In recent years, homosexual and lesbian couples—though infertile themselves for obvious reasons—have sought the rewards of parenthood. They have either adopted children or, in cases of ex-heterosexual parents, have absorbed into their new relationship the children they already had. What will come of this no one can say with precision. The world has never known, at least on a broad scale, such a thing as homosexual "parenting." At a minimum the values imparted to such children will not include the superiority of traditional family norms.

Enormous confusion is sure to afflict these children as to who they are and what kind of sexual role is theirs. Hence the *Alyson Wonderland* series of books, whose titles include the aforementioned *Heather Has Two Mommies* and also *Daddy's Roommate*. The books, designed for children up to twelve years old, depict homosexual living arrangements as entirely normal—not to say a lot of fun.

Among the virtues the family is supposed to teach is fidelity, a virtue that is less applauded and socially reinforced today than formerly. Whatever the sublime promises intoned in a marriage service ("forsaking all others," etc.), any self-gratifying society such as ours has problems with fidelity and the constriction of human activity. But gay rights adds a uniquely troubling dimension. Fidelity in relationships is not exactly a cardinal teaching of the gay-rights movement, nor is it even the standard practice of its devotees. "Promiscuity," wrote the late Randy Shilts in *And the Band Played On*, a chronicle of the AIDS epidemic, "was central to the raucous gay movement of the 1970s." Patrons of Denver bathhouses reported 2.7 sexual contacts per night.[10] In a 1980 interview with a New York City gay magazine, Dr. Dan William, himself homosexual, complained that gay liberation had given sex a dangerous urgency: "Twenty years ago, there may have been a thousand men on any one night having sex in New York baths or parks. Now there are ten or twenty thousand—at the baths, the back room bars, bookstores, porno theaters, the Rambles, and a wide range of other places as well. The plethora of opportunities poses a public health problem that's growing with every new bath in town."[11] The problem finally revealed itself fully in the form of AIDS.

But the instability of unwedded relationships is the present point, and the homosexual relationship is by definition unwedded (like the increasing numbers of heterosexual relationships mentioned earlier). Homosexual or heterosexual, attachments that are not founded on firm commitment are more dangerous than those the partners purpose firmly to maintain. This is why the contractual aspects of marriage are so urgent and fundamental. They obviate, even if they fail to abolish, jealousy and anxiety; they enhance, even if they fail to guarantee, trust and respect. Fidelity, which implies the deliberate limitation of choice, is at fundamental odds with the idea that is at the heart of the unwedded relationship—that is, the idea of selecting whomever one chooses, whenever one chooses, for sexual gratification. Homosexual activists who note the fragility that easy, widespread divorce has introduced to heterosexual marriage are entitled to do so. Yet they are wrong insofar as they depreciate the value of solemn promises and of attempts, however unsatisfactory, to live up to such promises.

Lastly, there is AIDS—Acquired Immune Deficiency Syndrome—which kills. It is the sternest rebuke of all to those who would claim a right to sexual pleasure in the form of their own choosing. Despite enormous efforts to depict it otherwise, this great blight is much more often than not the consequence of homosexual activity. "AIDS," writes author Irving Kristol, "is not some kind of exotic disease striking at random. The AIDS epidemic has its roots in certain forms of human behavior, and it is this behavior that sustains and magnifies the epidemic. AIDS is a venereal disease that seems to have been born out of homosexual anal intercourse. Just how and why this happened remains a puzzle, since such a sexual practice has been with us forever while the disease is (or at least seems to be) new."[12]

However AIDS began, promiscuity has caused it to spread. Randy Shilts (who in early 1994 died of the disease) recounts the key role played by an airline steward, Gaetan Dugas, in distributing the affliction among his sex partners from coast to coast. Dugas's lust was insatiable. He told doctors investigating the disease's origins that over the previous decade he had averaged 250 sexual liaisons a year. Self-restraint was not in him. "It's my right to do what I want with my body," he said. Dugas's declaration certainly had a modern cast to it. In the end, his philosophy of life killed him and many others as well. Thus we see the double conspiracy of carnality—joy and pride in a practice never intended by nature, coupled with personal recklessness and utter disregard for others. It is hardly an impressive recommendation for a lifestyle posing as a glittery alternative to the gray, traditional version.

Therefore, the association of AIDS with homosexuality is played down by gay-rights spokesmen or sympathizers. The politically correct viewpoint is that anyone can get AIDS. Heterosexuals are invited to consider the danger to themselves; if they do, maybe they will leave off "gay-bashing" and enlist in the war on AIDS. "The well-established connection between homosexual promiscuity and AIDS must be ignored," writes Kristol, "lest a bias toward 'traditional family values' filter into public discourse," embarrassing those who instruct us that these values are sadly out of date.[13] It is far safer, and thus highly popular, to argue that AIDS can strike anyone, regardless of race, creed, color, or sexual orientation. Which it can—theoretically. In the real world, the one the theoreticians normally find so uncomfortable, homosexual and bisexual men, along with intravenous drug users, accounted in 1992 for 70 percent of AIDS cases. Relatively few women get AIDS. Those who do use intravenous drugs or else share their bed with a user or a bisexual male.[14] And the moral question will not disappear: Without unnatural sex, without promiscuity, would this great calamity have come to pass?

The danger here—it seems to me, at least—lies in viewing the AIDS epidemic as the wrath of God. This is a natural temptation that should be firmly resisted. No one on earth speaks for God; to ascribe to him specific thoughts and actions is, if not presumptuous, reckless. Moreover, too-knowing pronouncements as to the Almighty's will can give the pronouncer's words a pharisaical lilt, spoiling otherwise purposeful attempts to note the iron connection between actions and consequences. The greatest of all twentieth-century epidemics—AIDS aside—may be self-induced blindness to this urgent connection. An age of liberation seldom expects dire consequences from behavior; but nature—a commodity the modern age views as endlessly pliable—rules otherwise.

At this point we come very near to the core of the moral understanding regarding homosexuality. The author keeps arguing that morality speaks to the nature of mankind, whispering do this, eschew that, not on arbitrary, petty, spoilsport grounds, but out of concern for the harmonious interplay of actor and environment. If fire burns and water wets—in all cultures, at all times—that is how we will deal with such phenomena, on the basis of their thoroughly documented, absolutely predictable nature. We will neither try to drink fire nor heat our homes with water.

The notion of firm *human* (as contrasted with physical) nature is something the modern age finds exquisitely hard to swallow. A nature that is always developing, ever unfolding, alive and alert to new possibilities, poses no problem to the century's consciousness. But that nature is not wholly human. The sensibilities of the eighteenth-century Enlightenment, in whose shadow we still live, are attuned to a human nature that needs only liberation in order to reach its full potential. The institutions and prejudices of the past are considered devices of enslavement; they point not to what could be, but only to what has been. Enlightenment devotees (whether or not they recognize themselves as such) are impatient with the notion of a nature not essentially different from the nature in which our remotest ancestors gloried and despaired. There is no progress in such a conception—no forward movement, no emancipation.

These are all exciting and attractive concepts, to be sure, which helps to explain why they command such a following.

Yet whether they square with the realities of human existence is another matter entirely. If the old norms and truths are so laughably out of date, why have not the myriad attempts to flout them made humanity safer, happier, and more in tune with that higher nature we hear about? Why AIDS? Why murder? Why one divorce for every two marriages? Why carnality and sordidness? The burden of proof, with respect to the imputed joys of sexual liberation, rests entirely upon the would-be liberators. The new, evolving human nature they would show us seems to have become stuck. The sight is not pleasant—and not one bit surprising.

CHAPTER NINE

Crime and Punishment

We began this inquiry with crime, and to crime we now return. In truth, we have never wandered from the topic. Sexual obsession may be the badge of modern culture, bathing the period, as some see it, in a romantic haze. But outside the haze, and often inside as well, lurk violence and assorted trespasses against the citizen.

So it has always been. The criminal impulse baffles every attempt to stifle or sidetrack it. We noted in the previous chapter the first recorded experience with homosexuality. Murder, as our Bible-saturated forebears possibly knew better than we do, entered the world several chapters prior to sodomy. "And Cain talked with Abel his brother: and it came to pass, when they were in the field, that Cain rose up against Abel his brother, and slew him."[1] The matter is recorded thus in the fourth chapter of Genesis. It is a sparse account—the murder weapon not even named, though it might well have been a club; no elaborate plot hinted at; justice swiftly meted out by the all-seeing Lord; the first murderer packed off to the first penal colony (the land of Nod) where he builds a city and founds a dynasty.

In due course the duty to avoid murder became the sixth commandment.

It was not the Hebrews alone who received such testimony. In his book *The Abolition of Man*, C. S. Lewis lists among many other moral teachings some of the proscriptions against murder that existed in other cultures besides that of the Hebrews. "I have not slain men" is, for instance, the boast from ancient Egypt's *Book of the Dead*. "In Nastrond [hell] I saw . . . murderers," runs an old Norse account. Why in hell? Because the murderer, through the violence he commits, puts himself outside the human community.

No official dispute rages concerning the horror, cruelty, and illegitimacy of murder. In our time we have wandered far from the old norms, but not so far as that. Nor have robbers, rapists, burglars, embezzlers, and lesser crooks and criminals ever found our oh-so-tolerant society ready to apologize for denying their pursuit of happiness. It is only natural that particular crimes achieve in particular times more than ordinary prominence. With the Soviet empire in ruins, for example, we no longer worry as we did in the 1950s about treason and espionage. Rapists are another matter, owing to the importance the women's movement rightly attaches to respect for women. Prostitution vexes modern Americans less than it did eminent Victorians such as William E. Gladstone, who, upright Christian layman that he was, conducted a sort of personal ministry to streetwalkers, bringing them home to meet his wife and drink tea. The modern climate of sexual freedom, without destroying prostitution, has made passion easier to satisfy on a nonprofessional level.

Are the 1990s more barbarous and uncivilized than previous ages? The question is interesting but not very fruitful. No age is without its stresses and strains, which manifest themselves in different ways. Why compare 1990s America with Victorian London or Augustan Rome? The variables are too many and too great. Yet one thing we know: There are no golden ages of peace and security. Even the supposedly placid 1950s were times of strain. The spreading blight of juvenile delinquency terrified parents and teachers who feared a time when the streets would be ruled by black-jacketed punks carrying switchblade knives. Maybe these adult authority figures, ridiculed at the time for their narrowmindedness, were perceptive after all. The youth gangs of the fifties have turned into the wolf packs of the nineties.

We know at least two things about modern crime: (1) Statistical measurements show it is sharply higher than in the middle part of the century, and (2) its randomness and brutality are increasing—and with them the fear of crime increases. Has our modern understanding of morality anything to do with these phenomena? Let us consider.

Crime indeed is on the rise—there can be no mistaking this. We have more than once used 1960 as an accessible benchmark. Let us do so again. In 1960, according to William J. Bennett's *Index of Leading Cultural Indicators,* violent crimes—murder, rape, robbery, and aggravated assault—totaled 288,460, for a rate of 16.1 per 100,000 Americans. There ensued the "Age of Aquarius"—a time, according to the famous song from *Hair,* of "harmony and understanding." And its picturesque fruit? A violent crime rate in 1970 of 36.4 per 100,000. Crimes of all sorts in this period increased from 3.4 million to 8.1 million.

By 1975, the number of violent crimes crossed the 1 million threshold; it neared 2 million by 1992, in which year there were 14.4 million crimes all told. While population growth in the period was 41 percent, violent crimes increased by more than 550 percent, total crimes by 300 percent. In 1992, 23,760 Americans were murdered—more than 100 times as many as in 1900; 109,062 women were forcibly raped. State and federal prison populations quadrupled between 1960 and 1991. The U.S. Justice Department forecasts bleakly that, at some point in their lives, eight of ten Americans will become victims of crime.[2]

The most depressing statistics are those that concern the young. As Bennett sums up: "The fastest growing segment of the criminal population is our nation's children. According to the Federal Bureau of Investigation, the nearly quadrupling in juvenile arrests has involved not only the disadvantaged minority youth in urban areas, but all races, all social classes and life styles. Because the population group of 10- to 17-year-olds is going to increase significantly in this decade, the violent upsurge may actually accelerate in the 1990s."[3]

News stories appear to confirm this drab analysis. When reading of a random, brutal slaying, we have come almost to take it for granted that the culprit or culprits are teenagers. Always the young have made up the bulk of the criminal class, but now that class is broadening. Today it encompasses twelve-year-olds—sixth- or seventh-grade children; young enough for braces, for the kiddie menu at restaurants. Nor are these the street urchins of Dickens's time; among these grown-up twelve-year-olds are hardened drug dealers and sometimes murderers. Hardly having lived themselves, they already have taken life.

The incidents of crime that grip public attention nowadays are worthy of note. They chill to the marrow—random, often pitiless crimes committed by children. Car bandit shoots motorist. Mugger shoots victim. Such are the crimes that make us gasp (proving anyway that we have not lost our capacity for horror). Such crimes do not dominate the criminal dockets, yet they represent a callousness and a lack of concern that Americans fancy are new.

In some of the better-known episodes from earlier in this decade, car bandits in Miami bumped rental cars driven by tourists, shot the tourists, and made off with their cash. A Washington, D.C. woman was dragged to her death by gunmen stealing her van. In New York City a young tourist was stabbed to death while defending his family from muggers. A female jogger was jumped, brutalized, and beaten nearly to death by a pack of teenage wolves. Yet none of this amounts to what tabloid newspapers once called in full-throated cry a "crime wave."

The present wave of violence has a spontaneous, almost casual quality. Here are peaceful, inoffensive people seriously injured or killed for no cause at all by people who, if and when caught, seem not in the least regretful. We are painfully familiar with their impassive faces as caught by the television cameras—eyes betraying no hint of fraternal feeling, lips like paper slits. They appear almost like creatures from another planet: living, breathing, possessed of chins and fingers and feet, yet in the most important respects unconnected to those who watch them with wonder and fascination. If these creatures are outwardly alive, inwardly they are dead.

Then there are larger, bloodier crimes—deeds of vengeance perpetrated against society by killers hardly anyone knew to be affronted to begin with. The first such incident of note occurred in New Jersey in 1949: A war veteran ran amok, shooting people on the street and in shops. Since 1966, when Charles Whitman mounted a tower overlooking the University of Texas campus and began blasting away at pedestrians below, incidents of random slaughter have become a part of our culture—an all-too-common means of violent self-expression. A gunman angry at how his child custody case was being handled shot up a courthouse in Fort Worth, Texas, then surrendered in a television studio, where he was allowed to air his idiosyncratic grievances. An even more savage massacre took place in a cafeteria in Killeen, Texas, where the death toll was twenty-two. Post Office facilities are frequent venues for this kind of violence.

Stories of this sort excite a feeling of vulnerability: *I could have been sitting there eating chicken-fried steak and potatoes when the cafeteria killer stalked in.* This sort of incident happens not in high-crime neighborhoods but in places that normally are accounted safe, even calm. The very randomness of such killings creates a climate of fatal resignation (What am I supposed to do, hide in bed?) but sows tension and disgust. Parents of a certain age know with certainty that *their* parents entertained far fewer worries about random crime than do parents today.

Reactions to these violations of the social compact, and of every moral code known to man, have a flabbergasted, hand-wringing quality. What can we do—take cover? Parents teach their young children to avoid and, if necessary, to run from strangers. Though hardly productive of civic trust, such an approach makes sense in light of recent experience. Many Americans purchase firearms, especially handguns, or expand the arsenals they already have. The intensity of the gun-control debate proceeds from deeply opposed perceptions of how to keep the peace: on the one hand, distrust of guns and gun owners, and on the other, the idea that citizens may not safely rely on the police or the legal system for the maintenance of order.

The instinct for security manifests itself in other, less ballistic ways. From time to time students kill each other for trivial causes, such as the desire for a stylish jacket or pair of sneakers the victim is wearing. In 1990, according to the Federal Centers for Disease Control, 20 percent of American high school students carried guns, knives, clubs, or razors to school.[4] The answer to the problem, according to community leaders, was to employ handheld metal detectors in schools, to pry out and uncover smuggled weapons. The peaceable and law-abiding have been inconvenienced—made to feel like potential terrorists—because a relative handful of true terrorists has chosen to ignore the tried-and-true methods of self-expression and resorted to means of its own. Nonetheless, the killings continue, on campus and off. It is plain to see that the problem is not merely one of detection.

What else can be done? When two black high-school students in the Dallas area are killed within hours of each other in different confrontations, the community is rightly shocked and alarmed. It is widely suggested that "change" is essential. Clearly, it is. Yet what kind of change? And effected how? A boycott of hard-core, violence-exalting rap music is suggested. Another suggestion: parental "SWAT teams," representative of the community, that visit schools and serve as "extended families" for students. There is suggested a mass media campaign that advertises positive role models for students. But then the organizer of the campaign confesses his bafflement at what goes on in schools. "What type of environment have we created," he asks, where security comes not from knowledge but from guns?[5]

What indeed goes on? Are the size and roughness of the problem too great for SWAT teams and advertising campaigns? If so, what can we do to start fixing it? Perhaps we begin by confronting an unpleasant truth—that the problem is moral, a matter of belief. Is killing people right or wrong? Increasing numbers of Americans answer: No, killing and beating are not wrong—who says they are? (Upon being asked why he feels the need to beat up people, a teenage gang member in New York City replied, "Because I can. Why not?")

How does it happen, at the end of the second millennium of the Christian era, that so many can give such an answer? One reason alone is possible: No one has taught them, at least with any clarity or conviction. No one, having taught the lesson, has backed it up where necessary with the force of law and authority. If killers believed in the principle of respect for others, they would not kill. They kill because they disbelieve.

Our crime statistics testify shrilly to the awful truth that, indeed, truth has fewer defenders than in the past. Those internal checks that should be relied on to pin back the onrush of passion are softer, weaker now. Where they do hold (consider the extreme example of the Amish communities), crime hardly exists. The noisy, nosy endeavors of the police are unnecessary except in the broadest sense; there is little to police. The people police themselves. Their neighbors know with as much certainty as human beings know anything that no one will walk into a cafeteria and, withdrawing an Uzi machine-gun from a bag, proceed to decimate the clientele. What makes possible this spacious sense of security is general belief in others' rights and humanity. That cardinal belief has waned in our time, which is disturbing and strange.

Something else is equally odd: We seem unaware of the change that has taken place. Up to this point in history, no society with long-term aspirations has wasted much time empathizing with criminals. Clearly criminals have always been human—created in the image of God like the rest of us, if you will—and so entitled to basic human rights. But the truly important people, as the social order saw it, were the masses of law-abiding citizens whose generally peaceful habits made the commonwealth possible. The moral tradition of civilization protected these people (or was meant to) from aggression, internal as well as external. The protection of life and property was the rock-bottom duty of the state, its fundamental reason for existence. A state unable to shield its citizens from harm, or punish those who lawlessly inflicted harm, had defaulted. It had no business playing with schemes of social improvement and uplift.

Certainly this is the historic understanding. Nor is it likely that many of those who have weakened this understanding truly believed that to be the job to which they were applying themselves. Criminals have attracted increasing sympathy in modern times on the basis of their supposed helplessness in the face of forces that propel them into lives of crime. These forces included the social conditions in which they grew up—notably conditions of poverty. In Victor Hugo's *Les Miserables,* Jean Valjean steals a loaf of bread to feed his starving family, commencing a life on the run that makes him the object of relentless pursuit by Inspector Javert. Indeed, social observers of every stripe have long trotted out poverty as a primary cause of crime. If only there were better housing, better jobs at higher pay, a climate where all human needs could be satisfied . . . and so go the sociological ruminations.

But the correlation between poverty and crime is less obvious than it seems. During the Great Depression, when unemployment reached 25 percent and human want was general, the number of arrests increased from .25 percent of the population in 1933 to .47 percent in 1941. However, in prosperous 1949, .53 percent were arrested, and in 1990 4.5 percent. Yet these days are accounted prosperous times, certainly in comparison to the Depression. In addition, unemployment and welfare benefits, at a level inconceivable to the generation of the thirties, are available to help moderns make it through the rough patches. During the Depression, the old view of personal rectitude held such strong sway that many Americans, despite their physical needs, refused to accept welfare. The begging hand, as they saw it, was a badge of shame. It compromised the ideal of personal integrity.

Additionally, there is the racial explanation: Blacks and members of other minority groups turn to crime out of frustration with a system that has excluded them. This was a popular argument in the sixties, and to a great degree it remains so. One hears it less today, however, because often it is drowned out by the wails of pain from the black community as black youths wantonly massacre other black youths. Why do "victims," if that is what they are, behave in this way?

Whatever the explanation on which they relied, sociologists, penologists, judges, teachers, and the like began to smooth the once-jagged edges of their anger at the criminal. As excuses for his behavior multiplied, the severity of his punishment lessened. Prisons became "correctional institutions." The inmates were there to amend their lives, to be rehabilitated. Courts, including the nation's highest, began expanding the list of rights that accused persons might assert in defense of their claim to be excused. None of this was bad, in and of itself. The operations of the criminal justice system are not always marked by compassion, though America's record on this score is exemplary. Peter Kreeft observes that our ancestors were "more cruel, intolerant, snobbish, and inhumane than we are."[6] We in turn are less courageous and less honest with ourselves than they were. Among the proofs of our waning courage is our growing inability to defend ourselves against convinced and belligerent enemies. And our lack of honesty shows up in the excuses we offer for our lack of courage.

When the topic is the ultimate punishment, death by execution, the excuses multiply and put out tentacles in every direction. Clearly, beyond cavil, capital punishment's roots are struck deep in our cultural soil. "Whoso sheddeth man's blood, by man shall his blood be shed."[7] Foes of the death penalty argue that the Law of Moses mandated capital punishment for various offenses that modern folk barely even find offensive (e.g., "If a man be found lying with a woman married to an husband, then they shall both of them die"[8]).

According to the objectors, our understanding of good and evil has evolved since Old Testament times. If the stern old law is woefully out of harmony with modern perceptions, so are the punishments it levies. Likewise it is said that capital punishment coarsens the society that inflicts it, exalting retribution over reconciliation. The horizontal view of life, dominant in this half of the century, emphasizes tolerating, accommodating, getting along. Yet another objection is the finality of execution. Judges and juries have made mistakes before, executing the innocent and leaving the guilty at large. Thus a prison sentence keeps options open, as contrasted with a visit to the execution chamber.

None of these objections is unreasonable. Each, nonetheless, slithers past the central question, which is: Are certain offenses so evil, so monstrous, that society's only plausible response is capital punishment? Always, prior to our own day, organized society answered yes. It was a question of proportionality—that is, the punishment fitting the crime, in W. S. Gilbert's immortal formulation. The infliction of death merited death; the betrayal of country (treason), which aimed at the entire country's death, merited a proportionate response—therefore, traitors went to the scaffold. What a society thinks about life, death, and questions in between shows up in the rewards and penalties it extends. That is what laws are—marks of social value, informed by tradition on the one hand, or television talk shows on the other; by constantly shifting political realities; by religious testimony; and by the long, cool judgments at which societies arrive only after centuries of collective experience.

This idea of a collective view can make life hard for individualists. There were fewer of the lone breed in the days prior to 1960, when tradition and verticality were stronger forces. Marching along to their different drummers, in Thoreau's phrase, they often found themselves marching alone. Their hour had not yet come. The beatniks thumped their bongos and spouted mystifying poetry, with scant impact on the larger culture, which preferred Sinatra or Elvis and lacked interest in poetry of any kind. Hugh Hefner, merchandiser of forbidden pleasures, was an under-the-counter phenomenon.

Then in 1960 the national furor over whether California should duly execute a brutal rapist, Caryl Chessman, showed that historic attitudes toward crime were undergoing serious reappraisal. A decade earlier there would have been no such furor; the world outside California would have been grateful to see Chessman dispatched to another realm. But the Chessman case coincided with the U.S. Supreme Court's campaign (it struck critics of the court as such) to accord lawbreakers new protections (e.g., the unbreachable right under the Constitution to representation by an attorney) that society had not previously entertained.

If concern for social enemies was a social indulgence, at the time it seemed one we could afford. A little kindness to criminals seemed unlikely to land us in vast trouble; the crime rate was not alarming by the standards of the day.

Respect for the processes of law was general. No high-school student, save maybe in the remotest "blackboard jungle," took a gun to school with him, in expectation of major trouble. City streets were not regarded as unusually dangerous for peaceful citizens. The author recollects long, late, meditative walks as a college student in a city of 200,000; it never occurred to him to doubt his personal safety. No doubt, he could not take such walks today. *The New York Times* acknowledged in an editorial on the first day of 1991 that "many New Yorkers now think twice about where they can safely walk; in a civilized place, that should be as automatic as breathing."[9]

By the mid-1960s the long-anticipated dawn of social individualism could be seen on the horizon. The horizontalizing of our social standards and of the institutions that enforced the standards was under way. The old laws represented a collective judgment we were ready to abandon. And the culture of the sixties, as it emerged around the time of the protests against the Vietnam War, excused and exalted violence for socially beneficial ends.

The violence to which war protests gave rise was real enough—chiefly bombings and fights with police, with a bank robbery or two thrown in for expropriatory purposes, after the Stalinist model of seventy years earlier. By the standards of nineteenth- and early twentieth-century terrorism, the young Stalin being just one manifestation of these, the college campus terrorists, with their middle-class finickiness, were not profoundly alarming. Talk, far more than action, seemed their metier. But the violence, as is always the case, cost innocent people their lives and fed the perception that society was caving in on itself. It likewise fed the notion that the old network of norms and standards was a hoax designed to maintain the status quo and the privileges of the wealthy.

Having launched into elaborate apologies for high-minded bombers and rioters, one found it natural to soften old condemnations of garden-variety murderers and robbers. How was one to be sure these, too, had not been motivated by legitimate social grievances? In fact, the political terrorists lionized any number of murderers, drug pushers, rapists, and pimps, making them out to be heroes of the culture wars. Most of those so honored were black. Soon numerous middle-class whites found it impossible to consider faulting members of any "oppressed class." And for this and other reasons they have tended ever since then to avert their eyes from catastrophic events in the black community.

The events stemmed from what Charles Murray, the eminent author and social scientist, calls changes in "the incentive structure" as it existed prior to the mid-1960s. Over the succeeding decades, the welfare system became an enfolding mother, teachers lost control in the classroom, and the risks associated with crime contracted. Society, says Murray, "deliberately stopped putting people in jail as often," while legal protections for the poor increased.[10] What, one wonders, was wrong with the legal equality of rich and poor? Nothing whatsoever; yet, perversely, when it came it fed the perception that the law was something not to be complied with but to be evaded and dodged. As the appeal of crime increased, so crime itself increased.

The expansion of the welfare system, as Murray has shown so wrenchingly, offered black fathers the strong inducement to abandon their families, and mothers the inducement not to care greatly. In 1988, 60 percent of black children (twice as many as in 1970) lived in a household with only a mother present. The absence of a male authority figure, according to most authorities on the black family, has made for a permissive environment, one heavily influenced by neighborhood forces, including street gangs that offer excitement, money, and a sense of inclusion. The effects on young blacks have been calamitous, not to mention the larger effects on our society. A 1991 study found that, among young black men in the District of Columbia,

42 percent were in prison, on parole, out on bond, or on the lam from police.

What is behind it all? A shift of social conviction—in some sense, the most profound in our history. A shift from standing against criminals and viewing them as social enemies to feeling more than a little sorry for them, even empathizing with some of their endeavors. The black militant who killed a policeman clearly should not have done so. But, oh, the frustration, the blind rage that could be read in his eyes! The tattooed loser awaiting execution for the wanton murder of a convenience store clerk is certainly a disagreeable type—yet he is as human as the rest of us, and not without gifts. Norman Mailer, playing Pygmalion, helped turn one such convict into a literary lion and best-selling author, a status that the criminal enjoyed until the day he murdered a part-time waiter who had tried to inhibit his raucous behavior in a restaurant.

Sloppy sentimentality of this sort is the natural consequence of putting different species of behaviors on more or less the same level. If good is not infinitely better than bad, in due course we find bad exercising a new attraction. Why prefer good on its own terms when bad offers instant gratification—gold chains, luxury automobiles, and the like? Equality of persons in democratic theory is uncomfortably close to becoming equality in outlook and behavior.

Wait, though! Surely we still have our principles. Surely we are against murderers, rapists, and drug dealers. America's prisons are full to overflowing. This may seem so—but look closer. Yes, the prisons are full—but of prisoners waiting to finish the *short sentences* they are serving due to the crowded conditions we tolerate.

As the author writes these words, a seven-year-old Texas girl is dead, allegedly at the hands of a child molester who was released from the state prison system after serving eighteen months of a ten-year sentence. That is how we *truly* feel about the crime of child molestation: It is worth only 15 percent of the formal sentence handed down on the criminal (assuming the formal sentence was stringent enough). Deep down, it seems, despite tough talk from politicians about keeping the violent locked up, we moderns feel embarrassment and discomfort over the duty to rebuke and punish. And so it goes in all areas of life that supposedly are governed by the moral law. In order to rebuke, the rebuker—parent, judge, citizen—must be convinced he or she is right. Yet how is one to know anymore? Are not all ideals of conduct approximately the same?

The author's answer is an unequivocal no. All ideals are not the same. Some are better than others, and always will be. The attempt to demonstrate as much has occupied us in this inquiry almost exclusively so far. From this point on we need to talk of what to do—how to put right, against all the odds, that which has gone so woefully wrong.

PART TWO

Toward Moral Recovery

Humpty Dumpty sat on the wall;
Humpty Dumpty had a great fall;
All the king's horses and all the king's men
Couldn't put Humpty together again.
                                    —*Mother Goose*

CHAPTER TEN

Guideposts
and Donkeys

Here, to recapitulate, is the argument. There is such a thing as human nature—it is the nature of humans. Humans are thus and so, they are this and that. What is more, with only slight alterations, if any, they have been thus and so since time out of mind.

We know more today than our ancestors did—or at least we are exposed to more and various kinds of knowledge; we travel more; we earn more and live in far greater comfort than was the case even fifty years ago. But the basic *human* differences between, say, the Americans of today and those of the Revolutionary War period are negligible. Any reading of history and literature makes this plain. One reads Hawthorne or Tolstoy or Shakespeare and says, yes, this is how it is!

There is also an argument from the negative standpoint. That is, if we humans have changed radically from how we used to be, then we are wasting our time studying and observing our ancestors' works of art, their books, their literature, as these have nothing to teach us. In this sense, a reader of antiquarian tastes might wish to idle away a few hours with Aristotle or Jane Austen, but with no expectation of taking away something that might tug gently at his or her soul. As for Bach, goodbye to his soaring chords and spiritual sensibilities! Who needs them? Rembrandt's solemn merchants, Raphael's madonnas bathed in heavenly radiance, Goya's grotesques—none have anything to say to us. Why anyone should hang them in museums, save perhaps for study of archaic technique, baffles analysis. The wars of the Greeks and Romans are material perhaps for romantic novels or movies, but otherwise they lack all relevance to a nation that can produce one squad of Marines who, armed with the latest weaponry, could in seconds annihilate a Greek phalanx. The history profession should straightway disband; its members could more usefully sell automobile insurance than impose on us their out-of-date narratives.

Yet we know instinctively that this condescending, insufferable worldview is wrong. That in itself is no inconsequential thing to know—because the very dismissal of that worldview entails the use of the word *wrong*. The word, as commonly held, has an antonym, *right*. And there are other similarly paired concepts: "good and evil"; "truth and falsehood." These opposites remind us of the awful complexity of the life that human beings lead.

The human nature we know and live with in our skins is complex beyond measure, shot through with contradictions. Some humans, striving for good, do evil. And evil motives on occasion produce good. It is a great maze, our human life—the byways and exits difficult to discern at times, and the choices seemingly infinite. As one wanders along, one's eye searches for guideposts—indications of where one is going, and of who has been there previously. One wants to know how to avoid the stumbles and slips that are to be expected along so poorly lighted a route. If there is a high ground, one would like the directions to it.

Where, then, are the guideposts to be found? And for that matter, what are they? The searcher is more fortunate than he or she may suppose. The guideposts are everywhere—not simply posted at key crossroads, but flourishing in the air itself. A song, a story, a legend, a maxim, a painting, a book, a prayer, a warning, a word of praise—such are the guideposts. As we observe them, we plot a safe and in no way tedious path. As we ignore them, we stumble and sometimes fall.

But do *any* guideposts serve the basic purpose of our orientation? There are guideposts, and then there are guideposts. The ones that matter, the ones that count are those whose craftsmen have based their handiwork on the fullest possible understanding of who we are, what we are, and where we are bound. These craftsmen have understood human nature, in other words—if not in whole (who could ever do that?), at least in substantial part.

Not all artisans have shared or accepted this understanding. Some have denied the reality of a constant human nature, as identifiable in one age as in another, or they have imagined that nature to be something radically different from what had been believed until then. The signs they have put up in increasing numbers over the past two centuries are exhortations such as, "Do it," "Take it," "Enjoy it"—"it" being whatever object of fancy might lie beside the pathway.

Such exhortations sound like fun. That is part of our human nature—to partake of and to relish fun. But the melancholy record of the past thirty years is that the more we seek to "do it" and "take it," the more misery we generate for ourselves and others. Our present social grievances and anxieties—possibly the deepest experienced in all of modern history—result from following the wrong guideposts.

Again and again we have turned aside from the guideposts that most clearly and accurately describe who we are and what we need—and we have done so that we might follow the easier, "better-paved" downward path. The famous episode in Collodi's (and Disney's) *Pinocchio* comes to mind: The wooden boy's comrades are lured to Pleasure

Island with the promise of endless delight and instead are turned into braying jackasses.

On the good and true guideposts are inscribed statements about human nature. We call these statements the moral law. They tell us not just who we are, but what we must do *because* of who we are. The moral law has a mournful, sad-sack reputation—which is understandable in one sense (many moralists are mournful), and not at all understandable in another sense. (How is preventable misfortune to be equated with joy?)

The purpose of the moral law is not to inhibit happiness but rather to enhance it. It is hard to be happy, the moral law advises us, with a deadly disease, a broken family, a long stretch in prison. The moral law, if consulted by ourselves, our parents, or whomever affects us directly, might have spared us consequences such as these. But to the extent the law was consulted, it was seen as suffocating, tedious, and irrelevant to immediate concerns.

Of course I'm happy, the philanderer replies. What is better than endless, illicit sex? He has what he wants, so why should bluenoses and Puritans bother him? For one reason, the consequences of endless illicit sex pertain to all who are enticed by his example. He may attract hosts of imitators, and his actions and consequences will commence anew, only multiplied. This is not even to take into account the well-being of the philanderer himself, who is not well served by endless personal indulgence. Tradition would advise him to study that guidepost on which is inscribed the ancient story of Don Juan/Don Giovanni, a moral tale to chill the blood.

To be sure, the moral law is not a prescription for the sunny rapture that modern times confuses with personal fulfillment. The moral law does not ward off the misadventures of life as if they were mosquitoes. In truth, nothing wards them off. Yet it should be axiomatic that those who do what best suits their nature come off best in the long run.

The moral law describes those behaviors—it shows how they fit on the human form like a well-tailored suit of clothes.

The word *law* remains off-putting to our modern society, signifying a thing chiseled from marble like the tablets of Moses. The laughter from Pleasure Island makes a happier racket than muttered creeds and maxims. Perhaps that can never be remedied. A thing that is meant to be reverenced and obeyed, as is the moral law, often has a distant quality. Its essential kindness and geniality go unremarked. Yet what is kinder, one has to ask, than the rescuing hand?

The literature of civilization is full of tales that embody this bit of wisdom. They are there to be consulted at the questioner's pleasure. The task at hand is to see how moral repairs may best, most effectively, and most lastingly be made.

✮ ✮ ✮

CHAPTER ELEVEN

"Moral Fever"

One thing at least comes of crisis. Almost everybody concerned admits the need to do something. Temporization in the face of impending disaster ceases to be an option. We fiddle around and it gets us nowhere. *It's time for action!* we cry. As Dr. Samuel Johnson observed dryly, "[W]hen a man knows he is to be hanged in a fortnight, it concentrates his mind wonderfully." So modern minds have been concentrated by the developments of the past twenty-five years. Riots, mass murders, AIDS, family breakup—the list of disorders lengthens steadily. "The problems of the 1990s . . . are manifestly failures of morals and values," writes Robert L. Bartley, editor of the *Wall Street Journal,* a newspaper more closely identified with economic than with moral analysis.[1] His observation defines the task with some exactitude. The means that are relevant to the task, however, remain elusive.

What many Americans want, naturally, is a program—action one followed by action two (or, more likely, all the various actions at the same time). The spending of government money figures into most of these programs. This is natural because it is the way we have addressed our national emergencies since the 1930s. Americans are believers in national mobilization. By mobilizing the willpower and resources of this most determined, most resourceful nation, we whipped the Depression, bested the Axis powers in World War II, and forcefully attacked the social traumas that in our perception confronted us in the early sixties: poverty, inadequate education, deprivation of civil rights. The "attack mode" suited us well indeed, and there is sentiment to the effect it might suit us again. Have we not already declared war on AIDS, for example?

The techniques of mobilization are easily understood. First the organization of a committee—a National Federation for Reform, let us say. Then press conferences and reports, the opening of a Washington, D.C. office, and the hiring of a staff. A newsletter follows. Above all, there must be a program for change that can be debated and acted on.

There is much to be said for action programs. When a reasonable remedy commends itself to reasonable people, why not adopt it? A rationalization of welfare, for instance, is that it provides strong incentives to keep families together and children in the care of male "authority figures." Such a program certainly would render life safer and more orderly. But this is not moral recovery. It is at best an antecedent step.

What would moral recovery be like? Consider first of all what morality *is* in the narrow, practical sense: a way of behaving, based on a way of believing—i.e., belief precedes behavior. We act as we do because such-and-such a manner of acting seems to us proper and just. (And unlike sociologists and modern theologians, most of us do not agonize over the meaning of terms such as "proper" and "just.") Even criminals act according to an inner perception of what is suitable to their circumstances and needs. A network news program in 1993 addressed the problem of juvenile criminals. Why did they rob? the reporter wanted to know. "It's our money," replied one offender. Not quite—but the perception certainly is there.

And why is the perception there? It is there because, like so many other perceptions, it has been planted there. The culture of the past few decades has planted deeply in human soil the notion that crime stems in large measure from social conditions. One might reduce to bumper-sticker wisdom a large part of the criminological scholarship of the twentieth century with the simple exhortation: "Fight crime: Reduce poverty."

Yet the most concentrated attack on poverty in human history, launched by the U.S. government in the 1960s, has reduced neither poverty nor crime. Certainly we need prisons. More appealing all the time is the notion of boot camps for juvenile offenders who hup-two-three-four at the command of drill sergeants and run rigorous obstacle courses with packs on their backs. The idea is to establish unmistakably that in real life one's personal standards and expectations alone do not suffice; there are external—societal—expectations that must be acknowledged and respected. What a dash of cold water in the face this must seem to many: You mean others expect something of me? Hmm. Not all offenders will be impressed; perhaps only a few may. But for these few the experience of forced conformity could prove rehabilitative.

Yet clearly this is not the whole of the matter. After all, where do such "external expectations" come from, and what right have people to entertain them? What has all this to do with *me*, with *my* life and wants and urges? A crucial connection is lacking.

Always before, society supplied that connection through its great teaching institutions—church, family, school. Today, each of these institutions in its teaching mission has been disabled (or has disabled itself). Yet the broken, disordered condition of our institutions, however deplorable, does not change a basic fact about each of them—that belief is crucial. Unless prompted by right belief, right action may come to nothing at all. What good is a well-financed program unbuttressed by solid teaching and believing?

A recent well-meaning newspaper editorial attributed outbreaks of public mayhem to "young people with an inadequate education and inadequate supervision, on the streets and up to no good." The editorial urged "more parenting and mentoring programs" for the violence prone. That much would certainly seem indicated. But then what? What would involved parents and mentors actually *say* to these inadequately educated and supervised young people? The editorial writer's assumption was that they would say all the right things about social obligation, the peaceful resolution of grievances, etc. But there is one terrible possibility—that these particular parents and mentors may not themselves have been taught the symmetry and workings of the moral code, and may end up babbling no more than vague disapproval. In fact this seems likely, given the varied institutional failures of recent years. Many such programs of this nature address only the symptoms rather than the disease, in effect becoming fever caplets for bronchial pneumonia.

The only effective tonic for moral sickness is . . . moral teaching. Suppose we once again begin to think of crime not as romantic or liberating, but as mean, rotten, lowdown, a violation of one's neighbor's rights and an affront to God. The old culture—the one that perished in the *Goetterdammerung* of the sixties—taught these lessons with some diligence. But over the succeeding years the message eroded so much that one could barely make out the lettering. This depressing trend culminated in what might be called the Criminal Liberation Movement. The law-breaking gained both legal and propaganda advantages over the law-abiding. This odd and terrifying result fit in with the sociological quest to extend the reach of secular justice. The consequence, however, was the extension of *injustice*. The law-abiding rightly saw themselves beset *because* they were law-abiding. Their prosperity and peaceful ways made them easy marks.

Suppose the trend to be reversible. Where do we start—with prisons and programs? Rather, we start with minds. To be sure, this kind of work is more frustrating than bricks-and-mortar expedients that can be advertised, touched, paid for by taxpayers' money.

Belief, much more than policemen, kept the peace earlier in our culture, and not just in the pleasant purlieus of blushing, middle-class America. The columnist Walter Williams writes of the tough, inner-city Philadelphia neighborhood where he grew up, and of the personalities who kept the peace there: "Ladies like Mrs. [Dorothy I.] Rice . . . were the leavening and stabilizing factor in black neighborhoods of yesterday. They had absolutely no reservation or fear in coming up to a youngster and demanding that he behave himself. At best the youngster would shiver in his boots hoping the matter would end there. For any would-be surrogate of today, taking the same action could easily mean assault, loss of life, or at the least a tongue lashing . . . by the kid."[2] Surely this is just the problem. With the disappearance of moral authority, founded on ancient convictions respecting right and wrong, the culture of might and appetite presently rules the streets.

The reconstruction of our teaching institutions is clearly the cardinal task of the present day. Yet the task is more easily commended than accomplished—for how does a convictionless society teach conviction? If we depend on our teaching institutions to impart morality, and our institutions' moral capital has dried up, is this not moral bankruptcy?

Not altogether, because our institutions have not failed altogether. They have staggered, stumbled, and on occasion gone to their knees, but none has fallen flat (although public schools are nearest to that humiliating condition). Church and family, both wounded desperately, display a surprising vitality and sense of commitment to the old ideals. Anyone curious enough to poke about in the ruins discovers this reality in impassioned letters to the editor that cry out in quasi-prophetic tones against the collapse of moral standards. One observes, moreover, the proliferation of groups, many quite large, dedicated to the suppression of pornography, the strengthening of the traditional family, or the overthrow of abortion.

The author would relate a recent experience. At a meeting of parents, held on a weeknight in the cafeteria of the local public high school, a respected physician was scheduled to speak on "Sexual Dangers of the Eighties." The topic was certainly arresting, yet the crowd that turned out was only half as large as at the previous such gathering, when the topic was teenagers and cars. The doctor's lecture, accompanied by graphic color slides, dealt with the hideous dangers of sexually transmitted diseases. These, she reported, now abound in America; they include not just AIDS, but chlamydia, herpes, syphilis, human papilloma virus, and a dozen-and-a-half more. The doctor would hear none of the currently popular babble about the harmlessness of "protected" sex—sex with condoms. She dwelt long on the fearful diseases and unexpected pregnancies to which teenagers, their pockets and purses overflowing with condoms, are subject in the flush of romantic discovery.

The author has never sat in a more raptly attentive audience. With no shadow of embarrassment, the physician proclaimed the unfashionable, politically incorrect doctrine of premarital abstinence from sex. Her voice disappeared momentarily beneath a wave of—applause! On that evening a certified expert—an authority—had said the unsayable, had advocated not self-fulfillment but self-abnegation, the sacrifice rather than the appeasement of appetite. And an audience of middle- to upper-middle-class parents had found the experience thrilling. Their numbers mattered less than their fighting spirit. Anxious questions bubbled from the audience. How could they make sure such a message as this received the widest possible distribution?

(By applying to school authorities and, where possible, to private groups.) Just how often could the doctor herself speak with groups of high school students? (Once a week.)

The author, in his mind's eye, saw the old culture suddenly start to rise—slowly, hobbled still by some thirty years of pain—from the crouching position to which the spirit of the new age had beaten it. Moral traditionalists in America have not gone quietly. In fact, they have not gone. The excesses of the present seem to inspirit at the same moment they depress. Something may be in the wind. The novelist Tom Wolfe, chronicler of cultural hubris, has termed the nineties a decade of "moral fever," though he cautions that the "inflammation" may not last.[3] Perhaps it won't. And then, perhaps it will.

What happens from this point onward depends in large degree on our teaching institutions. And what happens with our teaching institutions depends on the reflexes and the courage of our culture.

And not on government? No. Government, though it may finance and operate public schools, cannot be considered a teaching institution. In fact, most problems with government start at the moment those who govern begin to imagine their mission is moral as well as administrative. This is not to suggest that politics and morality are strangers. A virtuous, upright people is likelier than a corrupt and slothful one to guard the integrity of its institutions. Inevitably, given that frame of reference, it is not only possible but necessary sometimes to frame a political debate in moral terms. A campaign to blunt the electoral prospects of a budding Hitler, for example, would qualify as moral. And all who share the position that human life should be protected would view as intensely moral a congressional vote to eliminate access to abortion.

Yet much of the time, practical daily politics and transcendent morality sit uneasily together. Government is (and was originally contrived to be) largely an administrative enterprise. Granted, there are different subjective theories of administration. Not all are wise, on demonstrable evidence, and not all are prudent. Yet to claim that one administrative theory is inherently virtuous and another evil is to go farther than most Americans are prepared to go. The genius of democratic politics is the accommodation of varied interest groups that agree to sacrifice specific goals and objectives in return for civic peace. This means, practically speaking, that politicians tend to shy away from moral questions they hardly are equipped by temperament and philosophy to handle. Abortion became a political issue through the intervention not of elected politicians but of unelected judges.

As for consumer preference in its purest economic form, here again morality speaks softly, to the extent that it speaks at all. What is a "moral" purchase or investment? What is an immoral one? Clearly an economic decision that defrauds another amounts to robbery; but robbery is not the topic. The topic is the billions of daily trades through which buyers and sellers exchange value. The buyer values a particular car; the dealer values the buyer's money. The deal is done. Both parties presumably are satisfied. There is no need to inquire into the state of their souls. Morality enters into commercial exchange when a party, say, boycotts or supports a "socially responsible" company through purchase of its products. Supporters of "animal rights," for instance, crusade against the purchase of fur coats and in some cases the eating of meat. The author himself confesses to having transported moral principles into the marketplace. For most of his life he refused to buy any product made in any Communist country whatsoever, lest his dollars, in however infinitesimal a fashion, contribute to the staying power of the regime. For similar reasons many American companies, under pressure from foes of the former white-controlled South African government, withdrew from operations in that country. The foes intended a moral statement about racial discrimination there through a body blow to the country's economic viability. Still, consumer preference is the driving force of economics, and there are no moral norms—e.g., "good" neckties versus "bad" ones. Rather, there are values (which change from generation to generation, if not in recent times month to month).

Among the big three institutions, if we may call them that, first in priority is the church (or was, until relatively recent times). The chief reason for this is simple piety. If God, as the Scriptures and creeds assert, created the heavens and the earth, then his must be the principal say-so in those domains. Down from the tip-top, metaphysically speaking, come the ordinances by which men and women are expected to live. These ordinances are neither fanciful nor arbitrary—they are framed expressly for the benefit of God's creatures. The church is to proclaim these truths, because they are, well, true, and because that is the church's mission—to speak God's truth in the world.

Next in priority comes the family: father, mother, and children, their relationship reflecting and furthering the divine design, their teaching embodying its tenets. The old Anglican catechism makes poignant reading in this "Do It!" age:

> **Question:** What is thy duty towards thy Neighbour?
> **Answer:** My duty towards my Neighbour, is to love him as myself, and to do to all men, as I would they should do unto me: To love, honour, and succour my father and mother . . . To hurt no body by word nor deed . . . To keep my hands from picking and stealing, and my tongue from evil-speaking, lying, and slandering: To keep my body in temperance, soberness, and chastity: Not to covet nor desire other men's goods; but to learn and labour truly to get mine own living, and to do my duty in that state of life, unto which it shall please God to call me."[4]

In due course, off to school go the children. Schools add worldly wisdom to the sum of children's moral knowledge. But this wisdom is intended to reinforce understanding of basic human duties and obligations. Church and family support the schools in this important endeavor.

Such was the relationship the three great institutions long maintained among themselves (notwithstanding the often scandalous gaps between theory and practice). But in our time the theory sustaining these relationships has broken down. The big three institutions, buffeted and undermined by the leveling tendencies of the late twentieth century, have lost confidence in their essentially hierarchical duties. In embarrassment and humiliation they have abdicated those duties.

Who are the teachers today? Street gangs are. Peers of all sorts. Talk-show guests, movie stars, professional athletes, news anchors, soap opera characters, bartenders, congresspeople, mayors. Not all their teaching is wrong or destructive. Nothing should inhibit a professional quarterback from offering essentially sound advice on, say, respect for teachers. But street and television pedagogy is, under the very best of circumstances, unsystematic, ahistorical, hit-or-miss, and unfounded in anything but the dispenser's opinion. This opinion some other dispenser is amply entitled to challenge. "Respect for teachers?" the gang leader growls. "Teachers are pigs." Who can argue him down as he glowers there, gun in hand?

From health care to immigration, no question among the multitudinous questions facing us today is more monumental than that which concerns the means of reinvigorating the big three institutions. Yet as we have noted, there can be no plan or blueprint. Here is frustration—and yet also opportunity. The irony of the moral revival, if it comes, is that it will restore verticality—not from above but below, from living rooms, church pews, and occasionally school desks.

CHAPTER TWELVE

✭ ✭ ✭

Heavens Above

Although our present concern is with society's three teaching institutions, a more immediate question begs consideration—that of the standards our culture is to apply. In modern discourse there are two kinds of standards: secular and religious. This is a relatively new development. Rarely before has there been a culture so self-consciously secular, so determined to keep religion at arm's length.

As morality is the heart of culture, so religion is the heart of morality. We must firmly fuse all three. Is such an idea strange or un-American? Not in the least. Alexis de Tocqueville, the Frenchman who was early America's keenest observer, found religion to be "more needed in democratic republics than in any others. How is it possible that society should escape destruction if the moral tie be not strengthened in proportion as the political tie is relaxed? And what can be done with a people which is its own master, if it be not submissive to the Divinity? Whilst the law permits the Americans to do what they please, religion prevents them from conceiving, and forbids them to commit what is rash or unjust."[1]

Yet this fails to settle the question. Why do not purely secular values suffice? Have they not sufficed for our culture for a long time? The plain answer is no, they have not sufficed. They lack the power to stand alone. Left to operate on their own, they totter. This was why the great Victorian jurist Sir James Fitzjames Stephen feared the spread of his own agnostic opinions. He himself would behave as a gentleman; but what about all those nongentlemen who lacked the guidance of that religion he spurned? He preferred to have his fellow Englishmen backward rather than lawless—an odd conviction for a philosopher, but not without practical results, as time would prove.

The very phrase "secular values" raises problems. It is fashionable today to talk of "values," things to which people attach value, rather than of norms and standards, things that exist independently. A value usually is judged a matter of opinion—of individual insight, judgment, or preference. It can be a thing as simple as a taste for cheeseburgers or as complex as a devotion to Kant.

There is no way to "prove" a secular value. If I say Woody Allen is the finest comedian of our day and his movies the funniest and most moving the film craft affords, I have offered a nonbinding judgment. You may receive it with appreciation, or you may reject it. This is your affair, and I must respect that.

Indeed, from the dawn of time human opinions have differed. The world is organized to assimilate varying tastes and preferences. There is nonetheless a new feature. We have projected "values"—consumer preferences, really—into the moral realm, where they are alien entities.

We have gone far already toward placing the full range of our beliefs and convictions on the same level—marriage versus divorce, infidelity versus constancy. We do it as casually as if we were pairing off Woody Allen against Clint

Eastwood, barbecue brisket against granola, saying, here, choose whichever you like, it's all the same, really.

Antagonism toward crime remains. Nevertheless there exists the impulse to excuse or downplay particular species of behavior—where the accused has suffered injustice or deprivation of some sort. This was painfully true at the time of the Los Angeles riots in 1992. "Rage" was the favored word for describing the emotions of the rioters who took over large portions of the community after a jury acquitted officers on trial for the hugely publicized beating of Rodney King. A San Franciscan interviewed by the *Los Angeles Times* said, "Yeah, it's gotten out of hand, but society has gotten out of hand. All this [looting] is a manifestation of all that pain and suffering. This is as permissible as what happened to Rodney King on the streets."[2]

A junior-high teacher who was watching it all explained: "This is a statement these people are making. What all this means is that we are saying that if our higher-ups can get away with abuse and lawlessness, then we are also going to be lawless. We are going to do everything we can get away with."[3] Thus black rioters destroyed whole sections of Los Angeles inhabited by fellow blacks, looting and burning out merchants on whom black consumers depended. Perhaps that itself was a consumer judgment—the psychic "need" for revenge, awarded priority over respect for lives and property. You never can tell what justifications will lodge in the heads of people who have cut themselves loose from the moral law.

What is wrong with subjective values? you ask. Do not such values lie at the heart of the democratic and capitalistic systems? They certainly do. And, what is more, we must make sure they always do. Democracy rests on the premise that an informed electorate, rightly or wrongly, will make subjective judgments—Jefferson over Adams, Roosevelt over Hoover, Reagan over Carter. A political judgment is subjective by definition; a matter of perspective and personal judgment, not to mention temperament.

Individual politicians and voters may talk as though moral principles were at stake in a given election. For instance, if Candidate A fails to obtain election, his plan to balance the budget will go a-glimmering. A balanced budget is a good and moral thing, isn't it? On the other hand, it could be argued that cutting back the budget too severely would take jobs from people, creating despair and family discord. Both propositions—pro- and anti-budget-balancing—are intensely subjective. One camp views economic responsibility as a spur to growth; the other prefers economic stimulus. Which outcome is the moral one?

We are left suspended in a web of "values"—none provable, none authoritative. We hold to values in the economic realm, in the political realm, even in the artistic, music, and literary realms. We are that kind of broad-gauged, tolerant society. But to bring values into the realm of *morals*, we object, is to court disaster! Morals determine not how we vote or spend our money, but how we live our lives.

The very value on which we lean hardest today—that of faith in individual judgment—becomes a candidate for disposal should the mood of society change. But principles of morality endure—they are built-in. There can be no plebescites on morality any more than there can be an election to choose the highest mountain in the world. We know already what mountain that is. Likewise, we know already from millennia of experience what standards for living life best suit our human condition. We know what works and what doesn't. The great tragedy today is that moderns have come to feel deeply uncomfortable regarding ultimate authority. What is our authority today? Individual choice. What did it used to be? The law of God.

The law of God both encompasses and enshrines free choice. Yet is also stipulates that certain choices are in and of themselves *good* and *right*. A larger "value" surely than independent judgment is growth in the stature of which humanity is capable.

What goes on in the midst of our moral tumult? The demolition of dignity—human dignity; our dignity. By dignity, the author means our verifiable worth, our stature in the created order, from apes to angels. He hopes such a matter is neither "secular" nor "religious," according to the narrow compartmentalizations we have adopted in recent times.

At present, we humans are engaged in degrading ourselves, sinking to mudsill level. Our very humanity is in danger. Our humanity? How can that be? We have still our photo albums and television sets, our bank accounts, microwaves, and cellular telephones—the proofs of mental agility that set us apart from birds and pigs. Let us recall, nonetheless, what humanity means: not just mental capability, but moral stature. Religion has much to say about the human condition in its fullness, a condition that religion ascribes to God as Creator. Now it is true, not every human regards himself or herself as divinely created. The author accepts the existence of the opposite view, while urging the value of the religious view. The value is this: If God created man in his own image, that makes man's position in the created order a high one—only "a little lower than the angels," the Psalmist assures us.[4] In other words, man is better than a wolf, an ape, a jellyfish (notwithstanding that particular men have been likened to just these life forms). Man's reasoning powers are superior. No horse ever wrote a book of philosophy. Likewise man has a sense of obligation to others; for instance, he rarely eats his fellow humans, and when he does, he is punished sternly. This means he understands, at least in a rudimentary or provisional way, the difference between right and wrong behavior. He may likewise appreciate the social incentives and disincentives that apply to different kinds of behaviors. The very existence of civilization depends on deductions like these. They distinguish man from the animals.

Both the Christian and the Jewish faiths, which begin with God as Creator, present this viewpoint in its clearest, most understandable form. Yet pagans, too—the Greek Stoics come to mind—have made the case for the superiority of humans over animals. The essential point is that humans should take pride in their humanity, which is special.

Yet if the religious view of man's origins is right—as civilization affirmed with near-unanimity up to the mid-nineteenth century—then religion is uniquely well-positioned to draw distinctions about man's conduct. Before rightness and wrongness can be acknowledged, there must be standards for judging which is which. For the whole of Western civilization, religion has provided the most reliable, and surely the most enduring, touchstones. These came from outside (or above) the human condition yet spoke directly and authoritatively to that condition. They still so speak, though fewer people today bother to listen.

The appeal to authority no longer sweeps aside objections and criticisms. We will discover this as we examine our teaching institutions—church, school, and family—and assess what has happened to them.

CHAPTER THIRTEEN

Back to Bedrock

Moral values at their best are religious values. There is no escaping this. And yet the extraordinary period in American life marking the 1960s through the 1990s has been in large measure the history of a people in flight from God.

This may seem a strange assertion, given that Americans remain statistically a devout and religious people. According to the National Opinion Research Center, 90 percent of us affirm God's existence. The Gallup Poll says 70 percent claim church membership.[1]

In population, America's larger churches are the size of small towns, with multimillion-dollar budgets, large staffs, and programs of immense variety, serving a host of constituencies—singles, widowed persons, businessmen, alcoholics, and members of dysfunctional families, not to mention children, teenagers, and college-and-career young adults. In many of these houses of worship the lights are extinguished only late at night, after hours of activity and service within.

On the superficial evidence at least, one could suppose our nation to be genuinely upright, that "city on a hill" to which John Winthrop, borrowing from Scripture, likened early Massachusetts. Yet countervailing evidence must be thrown into the balance. The United Nations Children's Fund has called this same city-on-a-hill one of the world's most dangerous places for children. The U.N. report noted witheringly that the American homicide rate, for the 15 to 24 age bracket, is five times higher than that of neighboring Canada.

What has our God-fearing nation become, we wonder, and what will it be like in ten years' time? A moral transformation of vast proportions has occurred in our midst. The standards to which we adhere in every area are not higher than before; they are dramatically lower. Only in a peripheral sense is the saga of the twentieth century a tale of wars and economic cycles, of technological advances and social divisions. This is the sideshow. The saga of our time is the withering of our religious consensus.

The point is not that Americans scorn religion—hate it, fear it, wish it out of the way once and for all. Rather, it is that we have squeezed religion half-dry of its juices. Though we may not have intended it, still we have done so, as if playing with a fruit wedge in a cocktail glass. We Americans of the nineties regard religion as a good thing, even as helpful; it is better to have it, we reason, than not. But do we believe it is a vital thing? Not really, when you get down to it. Good people can muddle through this thing called life, using their instincts. The old consensus, with its elements of fear and awe, is gone. Divine thunder has become a low growl on the distant horizon—its decibel level akin to that of an empty stomach.

In place of the old consensus is a new culture—the culture of niceness. Niceness permeates our present way of life. Our moral authorities—TV anchormen, presidents, successful football coaches, folk singers with a social conscience—all encourage us to be very nice to each other; to offer love, care, and concern. Their eyes may even mist over as they say, sing, or preach these things. This emphasis on niceness as the great palliative for human woes probably stems from recollections, as old as kindergarten, that niceness is the attribute people seem most to value in others. Nice people are invited to parties and dances given by other nice people. Nice people are popular at the office. There is nothing terrible in their eyes—not the fierceness of the old prophets or the gleam of attachment to a distant time. The nice are accessible, their hands eminently shakable, their elbows always touchable. They answer our smiles with smiles. You would not find a prophet smiling; more likely you would see him scowl. And that kind of behavior would not make him a popular candidate for student council or state legislature.

What does niceness mean anyway? Does it mean to fulfill every particular of one's marriage vows? Or does it mean that when love "fades" we should give each other a break and call off the whole thing? There is nothing authoritative about niceness. Nor do the authorities who speak to us about being nice come across as particularly authoritative (the successful coaches et al.). Rather than laying down the law, they seem merely to be offering their own "personal" appraisals. These are welcome and helpful. But for the regulation of manners and mores, something tougher is necessary—something that one feels deep down, amid shuddering and perspiration, is *true*.

Still, in the age of niceness the notion of a religious consensus is troubling. Maybe we are well-rid of such a consensus. Do we really want the whole nation confessing the truth of a single religious proposition? If that is what religious consensus means, there has never been one, nor is one likely to emerge in our lifetime. The American religious consensus, as it existed until around the time of World War I, embraced holy rollers, high-church Episcopalians, northern Presbyterians, Two-Seed Baptists, and secular Jews. In a manner of speaking, it embraced even nonbelievers. This consensus rested on a belief in a God who had made heaven and earth and subsequently laid upon his people certain obligations regarding beliefs and behavior. Was such a bare-bones consensus the *theological* ideal? No one suggests such a ridiculous thing—only that this broad consensus had the effect of restraining certain forms of "wrong" conduct while inspiring and guiding "right" forms.

The American religious consensus was clearly not the kingdom of God on earth. It prevented neither slavery nor murder nor war, and certainly not sexual excess even among the believing. Is there any doubt that the Americans of those long-past days were people as we are today, with weaknesses as well as strengths? The American religious consensus addressed only those strengths—held them up for admiration and emulation and unashamedly used the language of praise for whatever was regarded as praiseworthy. There *were* praiseworthy deeds and attributes, yet also there were deeds and attributes of an opposite kind. In any case, the people of that time measured by yardsticks and calipers that were crafted not on earth but in heaven. Then they differentiated actions, behaviors, and attitudes. It was no use saying that this and that were the same in quality; they might bear a near relationship to each other, but they weren't the same, morally speaking. They became so only after democratic equality made its last conquest—of the moral realm.

The old consensus never was ethereal and distant. It was personal at its core. It taught, among other valuable things, a theology of the person in his relationship to God, a duty of obedience to norms and principles outside (or "above") the person, and a consciousness of personal sin. The Baptist might blurt out this sin in prayer meeting, the Catholic confide it to an unseen confessor in a dark booth. The principle was the same: acknowledgment of personal failing, measured against external (and eternal) standards.

One regrets that in the 1920s the self-appointed leaders of thought began to denigrate this old consensus and continued thereafter to low-rate it for its supposed narrowness, squeamishness, and banality. The old consensus worked, at least to a point. As we know statistically and not just impressionistically, the crime rate was much lower and the family much stronger when the consensus was in effect. Before modernism and the jeers of intellectuals finally overwhelmed it, the consensus provided reference points that no public philosophy could supply. This was because it provided the ultimate answer to the presumptuous (if human) question, Who says so? The answer religion provided was, God says so. Clearly such an answer failed to satisfy the nonreligious, who have been as plentiful in the United States as elsewhere. But the consciousness that God underlies and overspreads human life was common and broad-based. In general the absolute answer sufficed—that is, until finally the consensus broke up and niceness took over.

The culture of niceness has failed dismally and dramatically. We should not wonder at this, for inside the new culture there is little if any room for powerful and overwhelming judgment. The new culture, based on sensibilities and emotions rather than a foundational worldview, has not one viewpoint but a multiplicity. Beyond delicacy of word and deed and a commitment to virtually endless tolerance, however, the new culture has no idea as to what it should favor or oppose. Distinctions of this hard, forceful sort are not within the terms of its charter. The culture of niceness is squishy-soft at the core, timorous, afraid to say no, doubtful even as to when and where no is the warranted reply.

The old religious consensus may have been fallacious and defective at times, its ideas filtered through human understanding with all its limitations. Where were orthodox, God-fearing Christians, for example, on the slavery question? They were manning both sides of the ramparts, each party convinced its reading of Scripture was the right one. Card-playing, moviegoing, dancing—were these social tastes really the work of Satan, as was alleged from many a Protestant pulpit? Indeed, what of narrow, nosy, snooping religiosity that led to loveless condemnation of people who were only as blameless or as blamable as their accusers? Hypocrites have forever settled into pews on Sunday alongside authentic lovers of God, while here and there otherwise godly men and women have stayed home and worked in the garden. And yet, when the very worst possible has been said about the old religious consensus, and when all just accusations have been admitted and repented of, Americans in the 1990s must acknowledge that the old consensus helped superbly to keep the peace, both individually and collectively.

The consensus had both social and theological implications simultaneously. First, it spoke to means and ends, and it did so definitively. If God, as the consensus insisted, was the Author of creation, then the created beings he had called into existence were under vast and endless obligation to him. They would not hear his voice with indifference. This gave Christianity and Judaism to a lesser extent a marked social dimension. The obligation to love God with all one's heart and mind and, further, to love one's neighbor as oneself was, if nothing else, a prescription for social peace. But in fact it amounted to a great deal more. This was because religion imposed on the religious a sense of concern for others that went beyond niceness. This concern began with one's own family and extended outward. Churches founded schools, hospitals, missions to the suffering and dying. This was not just to be "nice"—it was to fulfill explicitly religious mandates. Had not Jesus said, "Inasmuch as ye have done it unto one of the least of these my brethren, ye have done it unto me"?[2] This was infinitely more than niceness—it was divine mercy.

Likewise, the religious consensus afforded touchstones of value. A religious precept was much more than a plausible alternative. As proceeding from the mouth of God or his designated messengers, it was an authoritative command. Love thy neighbor, remember the Sabbath day, honor thy father and thy mother, let him who is without sin cast the first stone—such declarations invited no back talk, no specious reformulations. Teachings, as distinguished from orders, took on authority because of their Source, that is, the One who had identified himself as Son of Man, the True Vine, the Good Shepherd. Adages such as "For what is a man advantaged, if he gain the whole world, and lose himself, or be cast away?" counted for much more than advice. They were admonitions touching external destiny.

Reason might fortify and elucidate such a command, but no believer derives its authority from mere intellectual assent. That might be the modern democratic way, with solemn assemblies convened to vote on divine directives— which to receive unquestioningly, which to appeal, which to ignore entirely. But democratic debate over God's ordinance was beside the point and partook moreover of insubordination. It sufficed that the One God had spoken. Whatever he said was right, ipso facto. And whatever he forbade was wrong. Whatever he said had continuing relevance—he was God. Nor could he be likened to some oriental despot, ruling by whim and intimidation. One always sensed purpose, as of infinite generosity, in the Lord's commands.

Morality was never an end in itself. Rather, it was a signpost, divinely placed and maintained. Moral behavior was behavior agreeable with the nature of the created being, and therefore highly advisable, as against behavior that depleted one's humanity. The moral choice fulfilled our nature and sped us toward a higher, more exalted relationship with the Creator.

Naturally, there existed in the grand design and its summation of duties "gray areas." These were considerable. There would be a constant and continuing need throughout the ages for teachers. And, indeed, reason made its distinct contributions to the understanding of morality. It showed the intimate relationship of human nature and moral prescription. The relationship could be expressed simply—morality is good for you.

This made sense. From the perspective of the religious consensus, a God who enjoined on his creatures a certain standard of moral performance would see to it that those who complied did not ultimately come off worse than if they hadn't. The Creator-God was not given to cruel jokes. Granted, moral behavior has never been guaranteed to increase job security or social standing. Joe Dokes sees his supervisor stealing from the company; he reports the rogue. The rogue, it turns out, is the employer's nephew. So long, Joe. He has done virtuously, but at no light cost to himself.

An entire school of popular theology addresses the question of why bad things happen to good people—people whose behavior would seem to entitle them to better treatment. According to the religious view of life, it is the Fall from Eden that has thwarted humanity's path to virtue. Yet the path of virtue, for all the rough terrain through which it runs, remains knowable. It is well-lighted, clearly delineated. Anyone can attempt the journey. It is all a matter of following the commandments, the precepts, the parables.

Even the nonreligious (not to mention the antireligious) profited from the old religious consensus, although it might surprise them to hear this. The nonreligious walked the same safe streets as did the religious, benefited from the same charitable commitments, lived under the same spacious legal protections. Madalyn O'Hair is fond of denouncing public acknowledgments of dependence on God, but her freedom to do so stems from a religiously founded grant of religious tolerance.

So for now the consensus is gone. Niceness reigns. Yet it is not so nice a time to be alive, if one values life and limb and chastity. Suppose that we want somehow to rebuild the old consensus, to bring back religion as the great teaching institution it has always been, a source of inspiration and remonstrance? What are the prospects, and what are the obstacles?

Obstacles first. There are two, and they are large—and ironic. *We* are the first obstacle. The churches are the second.

It might be said that we, the nice people of occasionally nice America are more an *unwitting* obstacle. Did we really intend to overthrow the old religious consensus? Not necessarily. We esteemed democracy, yes. We liked the idea that over here, in a land of limitless possibilities, one person's opinion was as good as another's. We failed to comprehend that, in terms of religion, we were not trafficking an opinion. The matter went far beyond democratic persuasion. The religious view had been *revealed*. A thing was right in itself or wrong in itself. A vote on such matters was worse than impudent; it was futile.

There was a democratic affability about the old consensus, and this contributed to its undoing. The religious spirit of America was a broadly accommodating spirit. No one denomination had proved itself the *right* denomination. All had their long and short suits, and all were entitled to a measure of toleration.

From this it followed that even nonreligion, when well-behaved, could be incorporated into the consensus. Atheists brandished no torches, bombed no churches. As individuals, they were not "un-nice." Some, in fact, were as nice as could be. The same went for secularists of all stamps—men and women consciously living outside the institutional church structure, considering themselves to be just as decent and honorable as churchgoing folk. The consensus' placid acceptance of unbelief heavily reinforced the civil peace; however, it likewise undermined believers, as they slowly ceased to insist on the theological view of human nature and human duties in the commonwealth.

As the twentieth century progressed (or regressed, depending on one's viewpoint), religion became more and more a distraction—even, to some, a barrier to legitimate change. H. L. Mencken's tirades against the "Wesleyan" scourge, echoed by the intelligentsia, made the Methodists, once our most vital denomination, look deeply pernicious. The evolution controversy of the 1920s, climaxed by the Scopes Trial and the breaking of William Jennings Bryan on the rack of public opinion, crushed the spirit of fundamentalists who had battled the advancing secularists with a literal interpretation of the Bible. The nation, it seemed, was not well-prepared to receive such an interpretation, and the fundamentalists were not well-prepared for rejection. They slunk away to their seminaries and churches, and the semi-pop religion of the fifties—the church as *the* place to be on Sunday morning—filled church pews without notably strengthening the moral witness of the church.

The 1960s commenced with the U.S. Supreme Court's rejection of school prayer and Bible reading in public-school classrooms. This was not just a constitutional novelty—there had always been prayer and Bible-reading in American classrooms, and scarcely anyone seemed to mind—but also a kick in the pants to the old religious consensus, delivered by our nation's highest tribunal. Millions viewed the prayer decisions as an affront to their faith, but the court's historic prestige had the effect of deflecting some of the anger.

When the author says that "we"—America's nice people—are a barrier to religious revitalization in the public sphere, he means that our long quest to overturn the court's decisions by constitutional amendment has failed. This failure was not one of political technique alone, but also of will. We nice people failed to try hard enough, an interesting circumstance in itself. Had we truly wanted the semi-secular, semi-religious petitions of that era restored to classroom use, the job would have been done. Our politicians would not have taken the high court's side against a people zealous on behalf of God's authority in public life. In fact, this proved true from the opposite viewpoint. When Madalyn Murray O'Hair challenged Maryland's law authorizing Bible-reading in class, huge quantities of supportive mail poured into her home, including checks and cash that amounted to tens of thousands of dollars. (This was at a time when $10,000 was a small fortune.) Clearly secularism enjoyed support at a level that would have been hard to imagine only a few years earlier.

Restoration of school prayer seemed to matter symbolically more than practically. The religion of the classroom circa 1963 was middle of the road—exactly what one might expect to find in the years when the larger society fused religious principle with good fellowship and niceness. We found in the end it was not nice to offend the nonreligious by offering prayers in their coerced presence. Niceness came first, prior to any efficacious results that might have been expected to flow from daily supplication. Since 1963—the cusp of the revolutionary period—judicial attempts to tighten the screws on religion in public life have enjoyed mixed success, but no real setbacks, either. Towns or school boards have been ordered to remove crosses and manger scenes from public sites and to prevent athletes, coaches, and ministers from publicly praying before games. Christmas carols and other songs tinged with religious meaning have been discreetly dropped from schoolbooks. The period of the Christmas holiday has, in many venues, been renamed the "winter holiday." Most Americans seem to have taken these changes in stride, having assimilated the secular understanding of religion as something largely extraneous to the world's concerns.

Yet here and there, particularly in small towns, religious people simply ignore the federal judiciary. They pray at school assemblies, football games, P.T.A. meetings, all but inviting the authorities to do something about it, and hinting that more may be afoot in America than is dreamed of in the high court's semi-pagan philosophies. Indeed, it appears that a remnant of believers may exist along the main streets of America, greater in number than the secularists suppose; a remnant deeply worried about the course of the world and prospects for their children's and grandchildren's futures. The cause of religious recovery will depend in large measure on just such people, the more so as their present ecclesiastical "leaders" stumble about in confusion, defining and redefining themselves. It was not "we the people" alone who did in the old religious consensus.

The churches' well-known, less-well-admired affection for secular politics is not the topic of this present excursion; however, it bears on the excursion.

The same symptoms that overtake the church whenever it contemplates secular politics are at work with regard to morals. Chief and most virulent of these is automatic deference to whatever is going on in the secular culture.

The secular culture calls the dance tune. Churchmen listen hopefully, expressions of peace and then delight spreading across their honest faces; at length they leap onto the floor, whirling their partners—the baptized membership—with secular flair. The music rises higher and higher, chords and harmonies clashing with historical sensibilities. The partners flag or flee. Still, parsons, preachers, and prelates dance on. In the strains of the music comes revelation. The revelation is that Revelation itself moves like the music of the dance—never still, always changing, twisting this way and that, so as to match the furious pace of Human Development. Catch up, catch up. The rhythm throbs in prelatical ears. Catch up we must; catch up we shall.

Of course the church never catches up. The culture is too swift, its movements too elusive for that. Whenever the church thinks it has caught up, it finds the secular culture only lately to have abandoned that corner of the dance floor. Still, the music throbs louder than ever; the clergy renew the pursuit, along with such partners as have not yet dropped exhausted to the floor.

The dance is not a pretty one to watch, nor is it inspirational. In the compass of thirty years, the Christian churches of the United States have thrown aside like an empty popcorn sack the moral authority they acquired over long, tedious centuries of witness and worship. Into the resultant moral vacuum have rushed all the cultural forces that were at hand when the abandonment occurred.

When certain theologians and other representatives of today's ordained clergy speak, it is hard sometimes to differentiate their voices from those of editorial writers, talk-show guests, and think-tank analysts. The topics, the viewpoints are roughly the same. Inquire of a clergyman concerning the propriety of premarital sex, and he may, albeit with reserve, introduce the subject of condoms.

The salaried bureaucrats, who look after the affairs of individual denominations, are in some ways the least qualified of all potential spokesmen for the members, few of whom the bureaucrats will ever have encountered in the way of business.

Herewith a confession: "The churches" is a gross but inescapable generalization. No one voice speaks for America's churches, nor does any committee of voices make a larger claim. Indeed, among "the churches," viewpoints differ on the imperatives of moral witness. So-called "mainline" bodies—Episcopalians, Presbyterians, United Methodists—are friendliest to the new moral currents running through society. Evangelicals and fundamentalists are the least friendly. Roman Catholics represent a variety of viewpoints, though the church's leadership—the most hierarchical of any Christian body—follows Pope John Paul II in opposing moral license.

Prior to World War II the churches sounded a more certain trumpet call. Mencken and his enlightened brethren, skeptics to begin with, proclaimed the irrelevance of moral standards in terms of the new dispensation. Yet the churches mainly held firm in their witness: Man was of God. God was in charge. He had stated his will. This will was reflected in the created nature of humanity. What most bothered the new twentieth-century men and women was the spiritual imperialism of it all; men and women of flesh, living their fleshly lives according to the prescriptions of the dead or unseen. The Sermon on the Mount had summoned believers to a higher standard than self-absorption. ("Seek ye first the kingdom of God, and his righteousness; and all these things shall be added unto you."[3]) But such an ideal, in a bustling century full of unrealized possibility, was difficult and (worse) undemocratic—monarchical even, when you got down to it.

By the 1960s, men and women were tired of being bossed. They lusted for self-realization, self-fulfillment. The plain truth was, they *lusted*. Amid exhortations to "Do it!" sixties culture kicked flat the old moral barriers, weakened by so many decades of criticism and suspicion. With a mighty whoop, the warriors of the new culture took possession. Accompanying them, oddly enough, was a host of volunteer chaplains, ready to consecrate the enterprise and proclaim that the stern, old standards of morality, having outlasted their time, should go as soon as possible.

It is not easy to say why this should have been so. If 100,000 ordained apologists followed after the mobs, there likely were 100,000 different reasons for doing it. There was fear of growing irrelevance: What if the "Do it" people turned their backs on the church, spurning potluck suppers and, worse, the collection plate? There was cultured dislike of people just a little too pious for their own good (though piety, you would have thought, was an attribute clergymen would recommend, over and against licentiousness). There was dislike of traditional culture, which viewed as a whole, was the culture of scribes and Pharisees.

Yet a common denominator seemed to link these liberated clergymen: They had ceased to trust in the revelation with which they had been entrusted. In an age sharply redefining itself, it made sense seemingly to redefine God wherever necessary. As our daily perceptions of life and our place in it grew, so our understanding of God had to grow.

Thus, today, homosexuality has its clerical defenders (as well as practitioners). Divorce and adultery no longer draw the spiritual condemnation they formerly received. Within certain denominations, pressure grows to lift the old sanctions entirely. Episcopal Bishop John S. Spong, noting "gigantic shifts in consciousness, values, and human power equations," submits that "there can be Holy sex"—including homosexual relations—"in the life of a mature single adult."[4] Other bishops undertake to ordain practicing, professed homosexuals as priests of the church.

A Presbyterian proposal in 1991 would have recognized "sexual relations in which there is genuine equality and mutual respect. . . . What matters is not narrowly whether sexually active adults are married or not, but rather whether they embody justice-love in their relating. . . . Homosexual love, no less and no more than heterosexual love, is right and good."[5] The proposal was decisively voted down after pastors and laypeople mobilized indignant opposition. Yet it is likely that those who, whatever their denomination, hold such convictions will continue to operate in accordance with them, awaiting the conversion of the national church. Meanwhile the mainline seminaries churn out new clergymen and clergywomen who hold precisely these "progressive" convictions.

Even crime finds its clerical apologists—clergy who emphasize the deprived rather than the depraved background of the criminal. Clergy are especially active in movements to abolish capital punishment. Abortion early on found many adherents in the "mainline" clergy. Yet not all mainline churches are as enthusiastic about *Roe v. Wade* as was the case two decades ago; there is growing discomfort that sexual liberation has failed to produce sexual responsibility. Abortion has become, not an intervention of mercy but, rather, a sadly commonplace birth-control technique. The Episcopal Church, for one, has backed away from its former reluctance to take sides as between mother and unborn child. The child now commands much more of that denomination's interest and concern. Roman Catholic priests and evangelical pastors maintain as before their alliance in defense of unborn life. (Catholics and evangelicals are, of all American Christians, the strongest in defense of scriptural authority and the truth of Christian revelation.) On these basic questions the mainline churches assume weaker, less forceful positions, which makes it easier to accommodate the spirit of the age on mere matters of morals.

Yet, as we see with increasing clarity, moral matters are not "mere." They speak to the very nature of man: his obligations to God, his neighbor, and himself. What are the prospects for recovering this half-lost sense of things? Decent, the author thinks. Not exhilarating, not captivating—just decent.

CHAPTER FOURTEEN

School Daze

America's respect for education is legendary. Thomas Jefferson called for a "crusade against ignorance," and his countrymen promptly seconded the motion. Private academies arose in profusion, free schools for the poor multiplied in the cities.

From the beginning Americans knew what they wanted their schools to deliver. Education was not about theoretical knowledge, it was about practical consequences, such as the imparting of patriotism and democratic values.

Horace Mann, who as secretary of the Massachusetts Board of Education is generally credited with founding the public-school system, saw universal education as a counterweight to "this tendency to the domination of capital and the servility of labor." The general diffusion of education, he maintained, would "draw property after it by the strongest of attractions; for such a thing never did happen, and never can happen, as that an intelligent and practical body of men should be permanently poor."[1]

Noah Webster wanted the schools to teach love of country. "As soon as [the schoolboy] opens his lips," the father of the American dictionary declared, "he should rehearse the history of his own country; he should lisp the praise of liberty, and of those illustrious heroes and statesmen who have wrought a revolution in her favor."[2] A few decades later came William Holmes McGuffey's *Eclectic Readers,* heavy with poems and stories intended to uplift and inspire young readers. James Montgomery's story about Arnold Winkelried has the Swiss patriot, at the moment of his sacrificial death, cry out, "Make way for Liberty!" Webster surely would have smiled approval.

More recently, federal judges have assigned public schools the task of breaking down barriers to a racially integrated society. Busing for purposes of racial "balance" in the classroom has often been the stipulated technique. Another favorite task is what we broadly refer to as "sex education." Didactic, tendentious, solemn—from the start American schools have been all these things. Deliberately so.

It is no surprise, then, to find tendentious, if well-meaning, people looking to public schools for help in the fight to reverse the moral trends of the day. The schools are in one sense a fruitful place to begin. All the woeful tendencies of the times are reflected there—exactly as one might expect of an institution whose values are in constant interplay with the values of society. We have noted already the violence that shakes and sunders many school campuses—attacks on teachers by students, attacks on students by other students, murders by students or outsiders. This is awful—and yet it is not even the whole woeful picture. American young people are victims and exemplars of a broad decline in moral standards. Two out of three teenage drinkers begin in the ninth grade. Suicide, once a rarity among teenagers, now is the third most common cause of death in that age bracket, after accidents and murders. Unwanted pregnancies in the mid-1980s rose 23 percent among children ten to fourteen years of age; among the same age group, gonorrhea quadrupled between 1960 and 1988. According to a survey in 1993, nine out of ten high-school students say cheating takes place in their schools; three out of four say students steal from each other.[3]

This audience undoubtedly is ripe for moral instruction. Whether the setting is right and the means are right are separate questions. But that schools can do *something* is plain. After all, that has been the American way. "Education reform," writes William J. Bennett, "is not an arcane business; it is not primarily a matter of great complexity, but one of will and political courage. It involves the willingness to hold institutions and individuals accountable, to make a commitment to each child, and the courage when necessary to challenge and change the system."[4] There are some definite success stories along these lines. Bennett, in his book *The De-Valuing of America,* celebrates some of them. But for the purposes of this present work we have to weigh the odds *against* as well as those favorable to the employment of public schools for purposes of moral revival. There is no use encouraging facile optimism (nor does Bennett encourage it, the author should point out).

Various considerations militate against overreliance on public schools as forums for teaching what a Massachusetts legislator calls the three R's of rights, respect, and responsibility. These are:

1. The nature of public schools has changed. That nature, as we have noted, is supplied by the society being served by the schools. This nature, in Jeffersonian times, was very different from what it has become. The society of the early republic valued the habits necessary to the construction of a new, muscular democracy. What was needed for the task of building the new democratic America were the virtues of patriotism, hardihood, and self-sacrifice. America needed citizens with self-reliant casts of mind—ready to open a shop, break ground for a new farm, or stalk off into the wilderness with only a wife and a milk cow as evidences of civilization.

They needed to love their country—for that was what they were building, a country. Patriotic tales of revolutionary heroes were the ticket. We recollect the Rev. Mason Locke Weems (the famous Parson Weems) as the author of a deifying work on George Washington. We likely fail to remember that, in addition to similarly lionizing Benjamin Franklin and William Penn, the parson wrote tracts with titles such as *The Drunkard's Looking Glass* and *God's Revenge Against Adultery.* Patriotism and virtue were of a piece. The challenge ahead for the new nation did not admit of participation by shirkers, cowards, drunkards, and thieves.

What are the odds of returning to a curriculum that teaches the old virtues? The author's guess is that the demand for such a curriculum is neither general nor intense. Again, the nature of society is not what it was—which means the nature of schools is different as well. The mind of the nation is more diffuse. We do not have before us anything like the single goal that animated Americans two hundred years ago. Rather, there is a multiplicity of goals: the healing of racial divisions, the overcoming of poverty, the acculturation of immigrants, career-training, baby-sitting for working parents, possibly even the transmission of culture and learning.

In 1992, when Colorado voters were considering a ballot initiative that would have given parents up to $2,500 in public money to spend on their choice of school, public or private, the chairwoman of the state education board was haunted by visions of schoolchildren, state vouchers in hand, decamping from the public schools. Winsomely she made the case for state-funded public education: "We seem to be losing touch of what public education is all about. It really isn't just about education. It's about people from all different backgrounds and walks of life and coming together and learning about one another. That's how the country was built."[5]

It is not as if the schools conceived of themselves as having *no* moral mission. Courses on sex and drug abuse are firmly embedded in the curriculum. The former are mostly explanatory, the latter hortatory. In other words, the education authorities have determined that knowledge of sex is good, in that it potentially prevents diseases and unplanned pregnancies. However, sex education is rarely if ever taught in a "judgmental" fashion—one that presents certain sexual behaviors (or their circumstances) as wrong in and of themselves. Exhortation is reserved for classes on drugs. Drug taking may be the only popular pastime the culture, generally speaking, regards as baneful. (Smoking and gun ownership are catching up fast.)

Nor are children themselves what they used to be—that is, relatively attentive, relatively disciplined, relatively respectful of authority, therefore eager for (or at least resigned to) the prospect of moral instruction. It would indeed be odd to find children more respectful of moral norms than are the adults with whom they live. A fundamental principle of child-rearing is that children gain from parents whatever sense they have of what is owed to others—friends, teachers, siblings, parents, and adults. It shows. A writer for *The New York Times* speaks of a "tide of truculence" sweeping through the schools.[6] The result, according to another writer, is "a severe erosion of respect among many young people for schools, teachers, and each other."[7]

An eighth-grade language arts teacher—not in the Bronx, but in North Carolina—complained upon returning to the classroom after a thirteen-year absence: "It's absolutely incredible. Kids have a real sense of entitlement now that you didn't see before. It's almost like a 'make me' attitude. It's not that they won't respect you just because you're an adult. It used to be automatic. Now there's a testing mechanism that goes on constantly. There are certain teachers they take advantage of because there are no consequences. We did that, too, but there's definitely a line that's been crossed."[8] This does not sound like an ideal environment for the teaching of statements about hierarchical authority—this idea, that book, or this course of action judged better than another. Authority, to be propounded, must be acknowledged. Such clearly is not the case in today's public schools.

2. *What authoritative teachings would commend themselves to the educational authorities?* This is no minor consideration. The cultural whirlwinds of the past thirty years have buffeted not students alone but also teachers. Thomas Sowell charges the public schools with attempts to "brainwash" students—actually to reshape their attitudes, "not only toward sex but also toward parents, toward society, and toward life." Programs of "cultural relativism," Sowell writes, have as their recurring theme that "what 'our society' believes is just one of many beliefs with equal validity—so that individuals have the option to choose for themselves what to believe and value."[9] Here is the same washing-out and blurring of distinctions that occurs across the board in society—the pulling down of "verticality," the exaltation of "horizontality;" the notion that every American is entitled to decide what is meaningful and worthwhile.

Sowell faults well-entrenched programs that undermine parental authority and present students as autonomous, wholly competent actors in a drama they craft to suit their changing needs and moods. Sex education is a part of that program, as is "values clarification." Here, one would think, we start to get somewhere. "Values" are going to be, if not propounded, at least clarified. Yet the "clarifying" process, once understood, dismays and discourages. The clarifiers are not seeking a "right" or "wrong" answer. No such answers, the student learns, are ready at hand. Rather, the focus is on the individual's feelings. "Alternative ways of constructing individual values, independently of parental values," Sowell writes, "are recurring themes of curriculum materials on the most disparate subjects, from sex to death. The risks involved in the process of jettisoning what has been passed on from the experience of generations who went before are depicted as risks worth taking, as an adventure, or as a matter of subjective feelings of 'trust' in oneself, in one's peers, and in the values clarification approach."[10] The voice of Jerry Rubin goes echoing through these sparsely furnished chambers: "Do it!"

Parents and parental authority come off badly in all such programs. The sex-education textbook *Changing Bodies, Changing Lives* presents parents not as trustworthy guides but as decided problems. A high-school class in Tucson, supposedly studying health, is asked: "How many of you hate your parents?"[11] Parents, when you get down to it, are people who tell you (provided they are doing their job) how to live. Wherever families are found, it seems power flows from the top in a thoroughly undemocratic, nonegalitarian fashion. One might as well live under the Third Reich! (Assuming that today's student knows the Third Reich ever existed—hardly a safe assumption.)

3. Schools today are only modestly successful at teaching what it is they say they are already teaching. Shall we saddle them now with one more pedagogical duty?

The steep decline in the quality of American education, as measured by standardized test scores and the encounters employers have had with undertrained, semiliterate employees, is well-known and needs no extensive documentation. A study by the National Assessment of Educational Progress says that many students read no more than eleven pages a day at home and in school. Consequently they fail fully to understand what it is they are reading. One fourth-grader, asked to describe an event he had seen, wrote: "One day there was a cat called Tom and a rat called Jerry they was a bad cat and rat the fight al the time they was a bad cat and rat the rat was picking on Tom the cat and rat all the time pick on each other the end."[12] This sort of thing exceeds caricature. The paramount emotion it excites is not disgust; it is sympathy for a youngster who for one reason or another has entered the fourth grade illiterate and most likely will graduate that way.

E. D. Hirsch, Jr. has documented and deplored the rapid drop-off in cultural literacy, which he calls "the oxygen of social intercourse." As a culture, we share less and less of the same knowledge. Harder and harder it becomes to talk with each other. "The complex undertakings of modern life," says Hirsch, "depend on the cooperation of many people with different specialties in different places. Where communications fail, so do the undertakings. (That is the moral of the Tower of Babel.)"[13] In this context, to speak of a young boy who confessed to his father the destruction of a cherry tree is possibly to raise extra-moral questions: Who was George Washington—and why do we care?

The question of how we came to this place is directly related to our larger inquiry into morality. We arrived at this point due to various experiences and transformations, not the least momentous of which was the egalitarian push to water down (if not to eliminate) standards of every sort. The anti-vertical impulse has been among us since the start: first in politics, then in culture, more recently in education (on which morality depends), and finally in morality. The canker of the eighteenth-century Enlightenment worked its way into the general consciousness: If all men were equally qualified as voters or consumers, so their various thoughts and works had to be regarded as essentially equal.

The consummation was reserved for that pivotal decade, the 1960s. Educational standards through the 1950s remained adequate to the realization of the country's scientific and commercial goals. The author's public-school education was accomplished in those times, so sunny-seeming compared to the intellectual twilight that shrouds the nineties. Teachers taught with diligence, and students received the knowledge conveyed if not with joy and enthusiasm at least with respect and courtesy. Every student expected to be tested on what had been taught, and expected his grade to reflect the actual (not perceived) performance.

All of this changed in the late 1960s. The attack on the culture was launched from the schools and frequently was fought out there. The radical demands of the day encompassed much more than Vietnam, and included academic "reforms," both at secondary and college levels. A recurring theme was that disadvantaged students—blacks in particular—were entitled to special consideration. They needed not only higher grades (to offset the burden of inferior educations received up to that point), but also special courses, such as black history, that better "related to" their identity and background.

In virtually no time, standards began falling across the board. Special courses of all kinds—black history, women's literature, movies, rock music—partly replaced the harder disciplines. In many schools grades were abolished or rendered meaningless. This was egalitarianism with a vengeance. And the quest continues. Despite a few modest efforts to restore standards in education, the egalitarian lust remains unsated. Its newest manifestation is the quest to redistribute property-tax revenues from "wealthy" school districts to "poor" ones. The theory is that equalization of resources will guarantee the equalization of educational outcomes. Yet the apostles of equality hardly seem worried that no correlation in the education realm between money spent and results achieved has ever been established. As Thomas J. Fleming writes, "[T]he pursuit of democratic equality in public schooling has only succeeded in degrading the quality of education and destroying the foundations of democratic life."[14] Thus the task of teaching moral norms in a public-school context looks formidable indeed. The schools have various and diverse missions apart from improving the character of young people. Present teaching methods do not lend themselves to the inculcation of moral absolutes. Besides, the schools don't believe in absolutes—which are the polar opposites of the egalitarian values now in favor.

But an even bigger, more consequential consideration hinders the ability of schools to address the moral crisis effectively. It is their incapacity to speak, even in hushed tones, of religion. The notion of public-school doors being barred to God would have confounded not only the founding fathers but also those who attended American public schools as recently as the early 1960s.

This ground has been deeply and thoroughly plowed. The author has no desire to pick through the constitutional perplexities heaped up around the issue of religion in public schools. Respected legal scholars have made strong cases for the right for teachers to introduce—tactfully—religious considerations in classroom discourse. Yet constitutional considerations aside, the author is struck by the oddness of the argument that separation of church and state requires the utter and complete secularizing of the classroom. If religion and churches are truly threats to our liberties, how did those liberties survive, and in such healthy condition, all those years of classroom prayer and Bible-reading? You would expect the imposing wall of church-state separation proposed by Jefferson to have been battered and beaten down long since, the stones hauled off and sold for church flooring. Yet in the years just before the U.S. Supreme Court's famous decisions outlawing official school prayer and classroom Bible-reading, liberty seemed alive and well. We had just helped emancipate Europe and the Far East, and the extension of full civil rights to black Americans was becoming the country's great domestic cause. The America of the early sixties was hardly a nation of gloomy theocrats, but, of course, it is difficult at any time to talk down justices of the U.S. Supreme Court.

A formidable task awaits those who would instruct students in moral wisdom without the advantage of drawing on theological insight. This is to tie one's hand behind one's back, and possibly to lace one's shoes together as well.

From what exactly does our moral crisis stem? From the modern preoccupation with the essential equivalence of all human beliefs, starting with the priority of self? If this is so, then the enemy is relativism. The student somehow must be persuaded—against the inclination memorably identified by Allan Bloom—that truth is not relative; that truth, in fact, is true. But now the question becomes, what are the reference points? Who *says* fidelity is better than adultery? You say *God* said so? Help! Get me the American Civil Liberties Union—someone just said the "G" word! And the howl for justice goes up.

There is no easy way out of this perplexity. If man is the measure of all things, then it is hard to argue convincingly against the right of man to do as he likes. Libertarians—whose creed is liberty itself—argue that man is free to do what he will insofar as he eschews the use of force or fraud against others. This is interesting: Maybe force and fraud in their own way are good things? One needs the theologians to argue otherwise—yet the theologians have been shut out of the conversation by popular or judicial demand. Secularists will not admit their claims to be heard except as matters of opinion.

Moral education, absent religion and its unique understanding of the rights and obligations of mankind, becomes merely a matter of shouted claims and counterclaims—what lawyers sometimes call a case of he said-she said. The problem is more than theoretical—it is practical and immediate. A case study may help to illustrate.

CHAPTER FIFTEEN

The Condom Cult

Among the multiple purposes to which the education system has been conformed in recent times is that of adjusting social attitudes toward the human body.

The chronology of sex education is worth examining briefly. In 1916, Margaret Sanger and her sister Ethel opened in Brooklyn a clinic that instructed women in the techniques of birth control, a practice then illegal under New York law. Already the Victorian order was crumbling; the Roaring Twenties brought increased demands for sexual freedom. The "reformers," as they styled themselves, had not yet found themselves welcome in the classroom, but the large social forces at work had begun prying open the doors. In the post-World War II period, the creed of sexual liberation, which had been stagnant for a time, began once more to spread.

Sweden, easily the most "progressive" European country with its cradle-to-grave welfare state, instituted sex education in 1956. The Swedish model spread to the United States, whose pupils were living in innocence of the liberation awaiting them. The author attended public schools at that time—from the late 1940s through the late 1950s. He recalls no course, scientific, historical, psychological, sociological, or otherwise, in which carnal sex played a part. The formidable body of unmarried female teachers who *were* the schools of that day would not have stood for any indelicacy, assuming that any male teachers had been fool enough to prescribe it. (They were not.) Our small-town school district may have dawdled farther "behind the times" than the districts in cities, but likely our approach was not atypical.

With the coming of the late sixties the old culture collapsed. The new culture welcomed, hand-in-hand with drugs and war protest, the revolutionary discipline of sex education. Just how much sex education went on in the sixties and seventies (and how much revolution came out of it) are matters hard to quantify. Certainly such courses were widespread, and characteristically those children who took part in them were initiated into the facts of life rendered raw. Masturbation, homosexuality, and oral-genital sex figured into classroom instruction. Students were invited to think of the varied forms of sexual expression as things of more or less equivalent worth. The counterculture was saying no less at the time, though saying it more belligerently. In some settings, instructors deliberately used obscenities and street talk in order to desensitize children and break down their old-fashioned inhibitions. This, too, was typical of what was happening in the broader culture. And that is why it is hard today to sort out the damage that sex education may have inflicted on traditional understandings of the relationship between men and women, boys and girls.

Consider the wreckage caused by television, the consequences of sex education, the influences engendered by friends and companions, the general looseness of the moral climate. How to distinguish among them? How to parcel out the blame?

We start by acknowledging that educational distortions were influential to a certain degree. Still one has to ask, which distortions, in which classes—literature, history, economics, black studies, women's studies? All have contributed in some degree to undermining the concept of authority and tradition as reliable guides to human action. While sex education surely played a key part in the corruptive processes of the time, it cannot assume unique guilt.

Neither does it help to blame the teachers of sex education. Where were the principals and superintendents when teachers were clinically setting forth the facts about sexual reproduction and pleasure? Where were the school boards? Where, most of all, were the parents, to whom all these other parties are at least nominally responsible? At the core of the sex education furor is a classic failure of nerve at the societal level. No combination of outrages could have taken place without the mute acquiescence of the school system's patrons, who are the parents. Whatever their moral convictions, the parents of that time were intimidated or shocked into silence.

This assumes that parents knew what was going on. Many probably assumed that the schools their children attended were proceeding in the same manner as the schools of their own day. Surely there were few instances in which the education authorities announced their intention to break down the culture's inhibitions concerning sex. It is more likely that as the earning of daily bread absorbed more and more of their energy, parents lost some of their former ability to oversee what went on at the schoolhouse.

It remains a given of discourse on education that the most successful teaching and learning take place in schools where parents are deeply, and often daily, involved. This sort of involvement still occurs in the nineties, but in nothing like the general fashion of the despised fifties, with their caricature moms in pearl necklaces bustling about the kitchen preparing milk and cookies. More milk, more cookies sounds to many like a useful antidote for a vast number of our era's dysfunctions.

That these dysfunctions are present at all is a fascinating point. What was sex education about, anyway, if not the conveyance of facts enabling children to take command of their physical selves? "Knowledge is power," Francis Bacon had famously opined—and what knowledge was more powerful than that pertaining to the body and its mysterious processes: semen, menstrual cycles, and the rest? The truth, it was supposed, would make children free to live out their sexuality in ways they chose themselves, rather than in ways chosen for them.

What do sex educators see, then, as they look around the schools? In plain view are the consequences of the modern sexual lifestyle: the bulging bellies of pregnant teenagers; the bleary eyes of young mothers who, in their unmarried state, struggle to reconcile the claims of parenthood and formal learning; the swaggering pride of fathers whose understanding of their responsibility begins and ends with conception. The awful (and predictable?) reality is that courses in sex have not helped to herd the docile multitudes to sexual utopia. Illegitimacy abounds and sexual disease is among the defining characteristics of our day. Margaret Sanger originally promoted contraception in order to free women from what they regarded as the necessity of abortion. She would find today, just three decades after her death, that the availability of contraception—while it may have helped middle-class women to "control their bodies"—has hardly helped poor women at all. Increased sexual freedom and diminished moral responsibility have combined, among other deadly effects, to make sexuality as much a prison as a field of opportunity.

The sex educators in their heyday were not unlike firearms instructors confining themselves to a purely mechanical explanation of a Colt .45's workings: breech here, trigger there. Yet you rarely encounter the firearms instructor so careless of his mission as to leave his students asking, "But what is a pistol for? And what do you do with it?" He would tell you, among other things, never load a pistol

human nature and destiny is outlawed in public schools. Few prospects so horrify sex educators as that religious people, with their idiosyncratic ideas of human destiny, might seize the lectern and begin walloping their Bibles. This would be improper by existing legal standards—an invitation to the federal judiciary to issue writs and remonstrances. Sex education cannot confront the basic questions—who (or even what) made man, to whom or what man is responsible, for what purpose is the replication of human life, and what are the responsibilities that go with replicating it.

All that sex educators can do is to clarify the mechanical details—leaving off any discussion of the mystery behind them—and wave benevolently as students leave the classroom to apply their new knowledge. No wonder sex education has so little to do with sex—that is, sex understood as the physical expression of human love. Core doctrines and ultimate purposes are matters for postgraduate examination, if anyone cares. We have here, in effect, an art course that stops cold with the techniques of color-mixing. This raises the provocative question: Why sex education at all?

Why, indeed? In part we have it because a now-large bureaucracy of sex educators has a vested interest in perpetuating even a signally failed experiment. There is a whole industry out there to keep alive—publishers, textbook writers, roving lecturers, classroom teachers. The industry has no use for the kind of downsizing that became popular in the early part of this decade. There are payrolls to meet and families to feed. This militates against acceptance of the heresy of moral orthodoxy. In fact the sex education industry must invent new missions for itself, such as preventing AIDS and teenage pregnancy.

The urge for self-preservation has been at least partly responsible for the cult of the condom. Back in the simple-minded Ozzie and Harriet days, few of the author's contemporaries had so much as seen a condom, far less pressed one into service on a lonely country road. Today, as AIDS and accidental conception blight the dreams of youth, the condom cult multiplies—loudly. Entire stores are dedicated to the sale of condoms. One such establishment, known as Condom Sense, is across the street from our family's favorite hamburger joint. No need to explain to the Murchison children what the store sells; propaganda for condoms is so commonplace that everyone today knows what only limited numbers of the author's contemporaries knew.

The condom cultists can be interesting to hear. They concede little to advocates of the historic and common-sense position that chastity provides chaste teenagers a money-back guarantee of their remaining non-parents. One response from cultists is, "Get out of here, you religious fanatic." Another is more complex: "Yes, that's true—abstractly. Abstinence would reduce pregnancies. But it won't work!"

Won't work? Chastity won't work? No, it won't work, the cultists reply: The kids won't let it. They want their sex. We can tell them abstinence is the best way—we might even exhort them. But they'll go out and do it, anyway. What we must teach is the use of condoms.

The facile assumption is that, while children should not be expected to receive moral instruction, they will soak up the directions for affixing a prophylactic to a banana. Chesterton's famous dictum about Christianity could creatively be paraphrased: "Morality has not been tried and found wanting; it has been found difficult, or embarrassing, and not tried." Perhaps the adults don't wish to sacrifice whatever reputation they may have for hipness by talking the language of St. Paul. What it boils down to possibly, is that the condom cultists cannot bring themselves to deny what has become not the right to sexual freedom but the *imperative* of sexual freedom. Throughout this toilsome century noble minds have labored to win that freedom, and while the victory has exposed the victors to perils they had not imagined—well, it would seem rotten to turn tail now. Ideology triumphs over reality; long live the almighty condom!

It is much more than this, and much worse besides. The condom cultists are not content with downgrading the efficacy of abstinence. They must also downgrade and belittle those who preach it. John Cardinal O'Connor, the chief pastor of New York City's Roman Catholics, writes that as he once waited to enter a church, a woman approached him and snarled, "How many kids will die in these streets because you won't give out condoms in the schools?"[1] Meanwhile, establishment educators castigate the "far right" for supposedly using family values as a slogan to cover up systematic assaults on the context of textbooks. The observation is meant as a reproach. In other words, the "far right" should not do such things, lest it imperil human freedom.

Condom cultists are fond of filing legal challenges to school districts that insinuate into the curriculum morality-based alternatives to a prophylactic sheath. For instance, in one Florida district, school officials were accused of violating privacy rights guaranteed under the state constitution. How did they violate these rights of privacy? By simply putting into place an abstinence-based curriculum. The problem was, the board was presenting abstinence as *the* right position, and, in doing so, was foreclosing alternative viewpoints, like the value of condoms.

The logic of the pluralism argument, however ("Let no position go unheard"), seems to extend only so far as it benefits the cultists. In Shreveport, Louisiana, for example, they prevailed on a federal judge to invalidate a sex education curriculum, only *one* of whose recommendations was abstinence. The judge found it constitutionally intolerable that Louisiana should interject "religious beliefs and moral judgments into teaching."[2] Since when, one wonders, has a common sense expedient become a religious belief? Clearly this reading disposes of the need to hear out religious enthusiasts pleading for their circumscribed view of a spacious secular matter like birth, life, death. This is a provocative decision, indeed, with provocative implications. So abstinence *could* work—by definition, *does* work—in a very practical sense; yet on constitutional grounds we can't talk about it? We have to talk about other, demonstrably less sure means of birth prevention (and HIV transmission). What a very bizarre notion.

Narrow, crabbed secularism of this sort the world has not known heretofore—certainly not in a society with the power and influence, as well as the religious antecedents, of the United States. The perversity of the "no religious doctrines" argument is staggering. Is it "religious" merely to state facts about the human body—that it works in a certain manner, and that in the natural course of things consequence B follows action A? To hear the condom cultists, you would suppose a statement of this sort to come only from a tribunal of Puritans in Geneva gowns, fresh from the latest witch-burning. No American has to answer Brother Jones's altar call or reverence the Blessed Sacrament in order to appreciate the sequence of simple cause-and-effect. The secularist mind may take in that same sequence, without blushing.

The condom cultists might merit a more attentive hearing had they a real solution to propose. They do not. Their "solution," in fact, is fallacious and deceitful. Condoms work all right—up to a point. No couple in the throes of passion can be sure when that point is attained and exceeded. A woman who depends on the condom for contraception has a 10 to 25 percent chance of becoming pregnant nonetheless. Perhaps the device is not used conscientiously. Perhaps it has a manufacturing defect (as do 10 to 20 percent). "The inescapable fact," writes Dr. Joe S. McIlhaney, Jr., "is that, during one act of intercourse, condoms *may* protect against [sexually transmitted diseases], but for frequent, repeated acts of intercourse over a period of months or years, *they will not* . . . neither the condoms nor the education programs about them are working."[3] Where is the safety in this kind of "safe sex"? The condom cultists invite Americans to play Russian roulette, using a piece of latex.

Meanwhile, the relentless emphasis on condoms focuses minds exclusively on mechanical techniques. "Safety" in sex becomes a matter simply of having the right equipment—stored, cared for, and employed in the right way. Sex in this sense becomes a purely mechanical activity, on a par with operating a lawn mower. The extent to which this approach to "safety" debases and trivializes sex deserves far more attention than it has received in public discourse. This is sex-by-the-numbers—joyless, depressing, a psychic dead end. We have no full sense of the damage the cult's campaign is inflicting on lives and spirits, because there has not been enough time to see the implications of "safe sex" fully played out.

The condom cult's message is only peripherally for younger married couples and the middle-aged; chiefly it is for the very young—the inexperienced and pliable. The cult is engaged in an enterprise of mental and moral conditioning. Its members intercept the young on their journey to adulthood, draw them aside by the elbow, and talk to them intensely. The voice of the tempter speaks seductively, in all times and places, telling the tempted what they want to hear, blessing the courses they are set on, assuring them everything is fine, not to worry, go right ahead. The condom cultists assure young people, contrary to physical evidence and moral experience, that "protected" sex resolves the various problems that have risen in recent years concerning the inalienable right to sexual freedom.

As for education? Of course we must educate young people about sex and morals. The problem is that the public education system, as presently organized and led, is an unlikely venue for the kind of learning that might make possible the arrest of moral decay. This is not to say the effort must not be made. To abandon the schools in this regard would be to abandon those children who can rely *only* on the schools for such ethical instruction as they get.

We must bear in mind, though, that of our three major teaching institutions—family, church, and school—the schools are the least capable, under present circumstances, of imparting moral instruction. This stems largely from their role as tax-supported instruments of the egalitarian state. Their job is to do the state's bidding. The state has decided for the present that raising moral standards offends the sensibilities of people who believe few if any such standards exist. Therefore moral standards are not to be raised.

For private schools, higher expectations are possible. These have the right to introduce explicitly moral and religious teachings into the curriculum. Indeed, they have the right to require of students a high standard of personal conduct. Nonetheless, private education saddles parents with additional financial burdens, and not all parents can shoulder them. This means that unless something akin to a voucher system* is enacted, the public schools will continue in the foreseeable future to educate the largest number of America's children. It is one more burden for America's families, who as we have noted bear large enough burdens now.

---

*A voucher system in its simplest form is a school financing system in which parents receive a voucher from the state representing the cost of each child's education. The school—private or public—in which they choose to enroll their child (assuming there is space, and the child meets standards) would receive the voucher. A private school could elect to participate in the system.

CHAPTER SIXTEEN

Reconstructing the Family

Ah, the old days—the fifties! With theme music blaring behind him, into the house strides Jim Anderson (otherwise known as actor Robert Young). His loving family greets him—wife, two daughters, one son—and in the succeeding thirty minutes, problems at school, problems with playmates and with boyfriends are ventilated and resolved, amid tears and good humor. The family—society's supreme teaching institution—succeeds once again in the context of network television.

However, the televised models of modern families tell us that times (and families) have changed dramatically in the three decades since "Father Knows Best" went off the air. We have noted already the symptoms of this change: an all-time high level of family breakup, soaring rates of illegitimacy, abortion, deep confusion over sexual roles.

Generalities about families are infinitely more slippery than those that pertain to churches and schools. There are all manner of families: black, white, brown, red, yellow; rich, poor, and in between; old and young; devoutly religious, or indifferent to anything that can't be seen; families with fathers, families without; first families, second families, even third and fourth families; "nuclear" and "extended" families (to use the terms currently in vogue); families loving, families antagonistic, families bored to tears with each other. To look at the variety of families is to be reminded of the variety of humans who populate this planet. What links them is the intent of each family's members to live, for at least a time, in a certain fixed relationship. A relationship implies commitment of some sort, strong or weak, particularly in the raising and care of children, who are the future citizens of our communities.

Of old, the bulk of families tended to hang together for various reasons: love, lethargy, determination, lack of opportunity, the social stigma attached to divorce, the religious stigma that underlay the social stigma. It is far otherwise today. Husbands and wives, in the spirit of the nineties, are forever holding democratic referenda on each other: Shall I stay with her? Shall I stay with him? Why? One never knows until the vote comes in. Such casual attitudes render the family's institutional prospects shaky at best. Today, a relatively stable home; tomorrow, perhaps no home. Such is the reality that increasing numbers of children confront. Under such circumstances the quality and quantity of moral teaching are badly impaired. There has to be, somewhere in the house, a stable platform for the steady inculcation of the once-familiar moral truths: Don't steal, don't lie, don't talk back to teachers, mind your manners, do your best at all times. Such truths require constant reinforcement. Once or twice is not enough. An entire childhood, fenced and framed by such teaching, may be enough—*may*, I say.

Yet there is still a larger problem when it comes to moral restoration. Moral teaching is authoritative teaching. Authority, in this horizontal age, enjoys nothing like the resigned acquiescence it received in the vertical era. An easy insouciance marks today's children—the raised eyebrow, the curled lip, the argumentativeness that is just short of rebellion, yet is a far cry from the automatic deference of yesterday. There is a mild cynicism about today's children that, if it existed forty years ago, was hardly detectable. Greater numbers of parents and teachers during the post-World War II period set out to mold children who would think for themselves. There would be no more barking orders at them, no ramming revealed truth down open throats. Careful, often tedious, explanation became the modern mode.

And what of those children who have not the slightest intention of being shaped, having begun life with unshaped or only partly shaped parents? Their numbers grow as illegitimacy grows. In the shaky circumstances of the single-parent family, where daily survival can be a challenge, the teaching of morality will not necessarily receive huge priority.

The broken-family problem, as we have noted earlier, is acute among welfare-dependent residents of the inner city. Comparatively little of the moral teaching and enforcement that Walter E. Williams found so reassuring in his own slum-neighborhood upbringing gets much attention these days. Williams's inner-city successors skip school and patronize rap artists who glorify violence against women. "These are young men," writes Shawn Sullivan, who grew up in their midst, "who themselves are likely to come from female-headed single-parent homes. Many have never had an older male figure in their family who could be there in times of crisis. They have grown up in communities that have devalued many of the institutions that sustained them in the past—schools, churches, and families. Most important, everything they see in their communities—especially from the drug dealers and gang members who control the streets—points to violence as the most suitable recourse for solving their problems."[1]

More and more journalistic accounts of the crimes committed by such folk speak of the criminals' unblinking indifference to their actions. They rape and slay without an outward sign of remorse or pity for their victim. So panthers and tigers slay: No hard feelings, you understand, they're simply hungry. Such morality as the criminal/animal might confess centers on himself. *His* deepest need—the need of the moment—has been appeased. The victim's needs? That is for *her* to worry about.

Do we see what is happening? The sense of human connectedness—which the moral code underwrites and enforces—is under grievous strain: at some points broken, at others desperately weakened. What *I* want is all that matters. Cain's famous question to the Lord of creation surfaces with venomous force: "Am I my brother's keeper?" Not in a culture that glorifies the sovereignty of the individual.

Three decades ago, the novelist Joseph Heller gave America's increasingly divided people what would eventually become a unifying byword: Catch 22. In the dark, bitter novel that bears this phrase as its title, an American airman during World War II seeks early release from the military on grounds of insanity. "Catch 22" is that if he wants out of the war, he couldn't possibly be crazy. Result: gridlock.

In a similar vein, the primary answer to America's moral troubles is for its primary teaching institution—the family—to begin teaching with old-time force and conviction. "Catch 22" is that the family itself desperately needs retraining. Retraining by whom? Churches and schools? Wait a minute: Don't clergymen and schoolteachers come from, well, families? Should *families* fail to hand on the moral law, then this newest generation of teachers and preachers may find itself as hobbled as its recent predecessors.

If children are to present themselves at church or school for moral instruction, then their parents must be predisposed to subject them to that instruction. But who predisposes the parents? At this point our head spins, our knees wobble. Visions of moral gridlock spread sickeningly before our eyes: In the midst of a full-blown crisis, all rescuers have been laid low, by their own hands or by others'.

And yet maybe not quite all.

CHAPTER SEVENTEEN

The New Counterculture

The late 1960s and early 1970s were shaped in large part by young people who called themselves the "counterculture"—the nose-thumbing alternative to the hypocrisies and sterilities of life as it was conventionally led (or was alleged to be led) in business office, country club, and family kitchen.

The counterculture had its own self-conscious manner of dress: blue jeans, often with holes in both knees, long hair, and "love beads." The point was to distance oneself from the culture of "materialism." Close at hand was a guitar, ready for twanging the liberating melodies of Bob Dylan, Janis Joplin, the Grateful Dead, Peter, Paul, and Mary—almost anyone save the likes of Frank Sinatra, Mantovani, or Perry Como, relics of a time being made over in the most public and dramatic way. If alcohol was the mainstream culture's "drug of choice," marijuana and LSD (lysergic acid diethylamide) turned the counterculture on, offering release and rapturous vision. No less liberating in counterculture-land was sex. Better yet, it was free: no obligations, no commitments to weigh down the participants—only endless joys.

And so it went, the culture and its values matched or mocked at every step by a counterculture with revolutionary intentions. These intentions it gradually enforced, not so much through the counterculture's great strength as through the culture's own lack of strength and will. Thus the counterculture, though unimpressively armed, won in considerable measure the battle of the sixties. It put to flight, or silenced to a whimper, many of the bourgeois assumptions that underlay the civilized tolerance of post-World War II America.

What has all this to do with today's culture, which reels ever more heavily from the buffetings of two decades ago? The point is just this: Now may be the time for a new counterculture (to borrow Michael Novak's useful term)—one to counter the culture of fear and fast-spreading confusion.

Let me be clear: What needs restoring is not the fragile, feckless culture that doubled over in pain a quarter-century ago when punched in the solar plexus. Why bother to restore something with such little power of resistance? We need neither that culture of niceness and general amiability nor the present culture of violence and stark confusion. What we need is a culture solidly grounded in the understanding of who we humans are and where we are bound. In short, we need a *moral* culture.

The author does not mean a culture of meekly folded hands and pursed lips. Prissiness and morality are not synonyms. Morality is a set of propositions about human nature. A moral life is one led in accordance with those propositions. By contrast, the ideal of the culture, as reshaped by the sixties counterculture, is the satisfaction of wish and whim, whether in accordance with our nature or not. In fact, the dreamy supposition of today's culture is that nature can be subdued or ignored. The headlines shriek tragically different tidings. We ignore the ideal of chastity within marriage only to contract unpleasant and often deadly diseases, or to consign the children of our bodies to lifetimes of confusion and stuntedness. We write off the rights of others at the cost of seeing our own rights written off by others acting on the same premises as ourselves.

Our proposed new counterculture has its work cut out. There is much to be done and, judging from the headlines, little time in which to do it. It might be nice, and certainly it would be fashionable, to pass a law—say, the Moral Restoration Act of 199_? And yet reform laws that proceed from unreformed hearts must be judged of questionable value.

True enough, from a public-policy standpoint, useful things could be done. An increase in the federal tax deduction for dependents might enable mothers to spend less time on the job and more at home. As noted earlier, a voucher system, affording tax-supported access to private and public schools of the parents' choice, might foster competition among schools, to the ultimate benefit of the consumers (both parents and pupils). The abolition of no-fault divorce for couples with children living at home might slow the rate of marriage dissolution—and, just as likely, discourage hasty marriages of the sort movie stars are famous for contracting. (Admittedly, such a law could quash the desire of particular couples to marry at all, lest they encounter messy legal problems, and enhance their desire to live together without benefit of clergy.)

On the other hand, it is better not to pin all of one's hopes on the enactment of even the most virtuous measures. Nothing is so uncertain as the legislative process. Today's hot notion is often tomorrow's dead letter. The kinds of legislation likeliest to gain the ear of lawmakers are those supported by massive numbers of constituents and opposed by relatively few. Of the three undoubtedly virtuous measures mentioned above, none as yet has a large and vocal following. "Vouchers for everybody" enjoys a large and growing constituency, yet also faces the virulent opposition of teachers' unions, which see vouchers as a frontal assault on public schools. "Oh, put not your trust in princes," counsels the psalmist. This still counts as good advice.

As the noted economist Glenn Loury of Boston University argues, "Sterile debates over policy fail to engage the fundamental questions of personal morality, of character and values. We do not give public voice to the judgments that it is wrong to abuse drugs, to be sexually promiscuous, to be indolent and without discipline, to be disrespectful of legitimate authority, to be unreliable, untruthful, unfaithful. The advocacy of a conception of virtuous living has vanished from American public discourse, especially in the discussion of race and social policy."[1]

If this is so, the counterculture must swing into action—in advance of the politicians, who always hasten to catch up once they discover what it is they have missed. Such a counterculture—traditionalist this time around, committed to the idea of right and wrong as objective concepts—has the large task of recapturing the imagination and conviction of all three teaching institutions: family, church, and school. These must be won through the power of ideas, which as Richard Weaver famously said "have consequences." There may be less resistance at the institutional level than one would suspect. If thirty years ago there was rot at the institutional core, at least there was a core. No one can find such a thing today amid the pronouncements of the self-styled intellectual leadership that dominates church and education and strongly influences even the conduct of family life.

There remains an obstacle of perception that must be hurdled. It is that vast public movements need recognizable leaders—headquarters; stationery; 501(c)(3) tax status for deductible gifts; computerized mailings. The old counterculture, on the other hand, which began in San Francisco, had no headquarters (unless it was the bookstore of the beatnik poet Lawrence Ferlinghetti and afterward the Haight-Ashbury district near Golden Gate Park). The movement spread because what it proclaimed and exemplified were the things hearers and imitators had been thirsting to hear, whether they knew it or not.

The modern counterculture must first locate and identify its moorings. On what basis will it confront a secularized society? Repentance? Society may not want to hear such a heavily theological message. On the other hand, did such a consideration worry the prophets and evangelists?

The larger point surely is this: Morality, if we are to reconstruct it in our time, must be anchored to some base. What base is more fitting than religion? There is such a thing as morality *because* there is such a thing as religion. Absent a Creator God, moral codes reduce to constantly shifting ethical preferences. Major questions are submitted to the arbitration of the electorate—each vote equal to every other vote. All in favor, say "aye." All opposed . . .

Thus policy is made in democracies, the fastest-proliferating governmental species in the modern world. Democracy contemplates timely policy shifts to accommodate changing needs. Do moral needs, then, change like balances of trade? That is what we heard in the "Do it" sixties. In the nineties we look about and a solemn realization dawns. *We have been lied to!* The ancient human appetites, torments, hopes, and fears are as before; the rewards the same, the punishments in some ways more daunting for their very unexpectedness.

No Creator God? Man, a figment of his own imagination? How does this square with the dawning realization that the moral prescriptions handed down in God's name have such awful pertinence today? The quest for liberation and self-gratification takes us by short, easy stages to death and malaise. Result is out of sync with theory.

The theory of man without God is the unhappiest and most barren theory human history offers. For a while, in the sixties, feverish hope reigned. Secular prophets, seconded by theologians of advanced proclivities, announced a "new morality"—a kind of make-it-up-as-you-go set of ethics that declared respect for others without establishing why others deserved respect in the first place. This make-it-up premise was fatal to the whole enterprise, however. If anyone could play the game, then anything went. The new morality—a term defined earlier in the century by Paul Elmer More as "the reconstruction of life at the level of the gutter"[2]—did not strengthen but instead weakened the family. It did not reduce sexually transmitted diseases such as AIDS; it increased them. Far from rendering homes and streets safer, the new morality encouraged criminals to explain away their pursuits as a matter of uncontrollable urges and frustrations.

As the moral debate invigorates itself, one finds many Americans resorting to noncontroversial categories when they speak of behavior as dumb or smart, safe or dangerous, legal or illegal. There is certainly truth here. Wrong things do tend to be dumb, right ones smart, etc. This bobbing and weaving to escape secularist reproach is entirely to be expected. Over the past three decades we have been educated by courts and pundits to think of religion, whenever loosed from the altar or pulpit, as a disruptive force in national life. This habit of perception will not easily be broken—nor need it be. The new counterculture can accommodate, in the democratic spirit, a variety of approaches to the goal of moral recovery.

There can be agreement, for instance, on broad premises, beginning with the priority of the family as teaching institution. And after that? What is the program? The basic program involves the general advertisement of the family's plight and of its quintessential importance. It is imperative to speak, in any and all forums, of the family's irreplaceable role in the molding of character. Character! A deliciously old-fashioned word. Let us use it until the culture turns blue in the face. Character-building is the family's essential job. Writers and speakers of all sorts—in print, on television, at the P.T.A. meeting, around the breakfast table—are to be encouraged in the diligent, unashamed use of these words and concepts.

The new counterculture must work to create a warmly hospitable climate in which husbands and wives lead lives of fidelity, and care for the children they have brought into the world. These stances of belief and commitment, so ordinary to our forebears and so quaint-seeming today, should become once again the societal norms, as was true long before Robert Young. Let us advertise these people not as freaks but as cultural heroes—carrying on the ancient virtues despite the ridicule they receive today and the praise that licentiousness wins for itself.

An "unconventional family," as an unmarried relationship is often called, should indeed remain unconventional—and unacceptable to the new counterculture. The partners in such a relationship will do as they like, but when they try to preach to the rest of us the normality and unexceptionalness of their "lifestyle," then the new counterculture gently yet sternly must rise and rebuke them. It must have no truck either with moves to create legal rights and protections for unmarried relationships, whether between men and women or people of the same sex. The spirit of the age not withstanding, such relationships are wrong on their face and destructive of the ends for which man and woman were created. We have always had such relationships among us and always will; but that does not argue for according these lifestyles formal or informal approval. To do so undermines the family's capacity, perhaps its will, to teach the contrary truths with conviction and optimism.

What a joy it would be to see the entertainment media once more celebrate traditional families, happy with themselves and happy in their pursuit of the good in life. Sometimes this happens, as with Bill Cosby's enormously successful series about a middle-class black family, the popularity of which should have proved the existence of a large audience for the traditional verities. More often the quest is for cheap laughs or shocks at the expense of the institution of marriage, which is made to seem the province of dopes or slobs, whereas the truly exciting (read: beautiful and sexy) people enjoy rapidly shifting commitments.

The entertainment industry, consisting mainly of television, music, and sports, is the captive of nontraditionalists who fear any "moral dogmatisms" that might drive off viewers and advertisers. Oddly, they themselves traffic in reverse moral dogmatism. The programs they present most often smile sweetly on unwedded bliss and, increasingly, homosexuality and lesbianism (and even crime, as in the case of some rap music). What can the new counterculture do? It can publicly excoriate the offenders, albeit without vast hope of changing their ways. More to the point, it can help to create forms of entertainment—TV programs, movies, magazines—that have a moral view. Such a view doesn't mean presenting elderly ladies in print dresses, but, rather, ordinary people wearing Gap jeans or business suits, battling the chaos of the present day.

The new counterculture must see to it that family and church reinforce each other: parents requiring of their children participation in religious life and setting for them the example of such participation; the church responding with soundly reasoned explanations of the human condition and its rightful bounds. One knows that the guilt of the mainline churches, in their attempts to accommodate the spirit of the age, is neither limited nor light. Again the judgment of Dean W. R. Inge, the great Anglican churchman, retains its full pungency: He who marries the spirit of today will be a widower tomorrow.

The spirit of the new counterculture will be thoroughly religious, the old counterculture having exhausted the possibilities of irreligion, not to say mystical and fake religion. But whether this spirit will again penetrate the public schools remains very much to be seen. The intricate connections between church and state, once taken entirely for granted, have sustained hammer blows since the early sixties. The effort to rebuild this relationship may have only marginal relevance, with the condition of the public schools sinking year by year: reading and mathematical skills generally in slump, illiteracy rising, lack of discipline increasing, sex education flourishing. The light, informal alliance of church and public school may be over. This does not mean the schools are forever incapacitated in the quest to teach morality; only that moral concerns in their fullness and complexity will suffer in a classroom context from lack of religious backing. This will be true especially if the new counterculture, through worship and belief and action, helps religion recover some measure of its lost authority. Barring monumental change, the public schools then will be thoroughly isolated.

This is not to deny the example of highly motivated, highly moral instructors who remain at their public school posts while the vessel founders. Nor is it to gainsay the teaching value of solid literature, as in days of yore (provided such literature is installed once more in all public classrooms and taught with fidelity and intelligence). Still, the public schools labor under possibly fatal defects, at least from the standpoint of their incapacity for moral teaching. Perhaps if the new counterculture thoroughly wins over the culture—including the culture of the public schools—the education establishment's newfound doubts about old-fashioned moral instruction will disappear. That is our best, if not precisely our likeliest, hope.

In the meantime, a more promising avenue for authoritative teaching leads to the private schools, many of which hold to religion as the norm. A voucher system that affords parents the wherewithal to choose a private school would reinforce the role religion plays in education, and thus the ability of the schools to rekindle respect for morality. (For this very reason, secularists will battle vouchers to the last.) If vouchers should be enacted at the state or federal level, the old counterculture fossils will doubtless seek to tie as many government strings as possible to the enterprise, possibly dooming it at the outset.

And yet . . . and yet . . . churches, families, schools of frankly religious outlook, financed by private means if public funds remain out of the question—here is no weak alliance. The new counterculture, with the aid of our great teaching institutions, can win back the moral high ground, and do so in our time before the last shoddy defenses against chaos come tumbling down.

It is a mighty challenge for Americans, this fight for the right—indeed for the truth. Yet clearly it is one we must take up with vigor. Not everyone cares to sit watching or cringing while the old moral order goes down. How did the moral order rise in the first place and take possession of us? Through the conscious choices of men and women of insight and piety to stake their lives—often literally—on the proposition that right is right in all times and in all places; not according to cultural mores and tribal norms, but by the largest of touchstones: the law of God, the nature of humanity, the experience of the human race. Those touchstones—damp with the cultural night air, unfamiliar from disuse—await our grasp, whenever it shall come.

NOTES

Chapter 1
1. William J. Bennett, *The Index of Leading Cultural Indicators* (New York: Touchstone, 1994), 8.

Chapter 2
1. Genesis 1:26–27.
2. Genesis 1:28; 2:17.

Chapter 3
1. P. J. O'Rourke, "The Forbidden Books of Youth," *The New York Times Book Review*, 6 June 1993, 13.
2. John Attarian, "The Deep Roots of Our Decline," *The Wall Street Journal*, 27 April 1993.
3. Crane Brinton, *A History of Western Morals* (New York: Harcourt Brace, 1959), 293–94.
4. Psalm 95:6–7.
5. Quoted in *The Eloquence of Winston Churchill*, ed. F. B. Czarnomski (New York: The New American Library, 1957), 15.

Chapter 4
1. Frederick Lewis Allen, *Only Yesterday* (New York: Bantam, 1959), 69.
2. Allen J. Matusow, *The Unraveling of America: A History of Liberalism in the 1960s* (New York: Harper & Row [The New American Nation Series], 1984), 303.
3. Ibid., 340–41.

Chapter 5
1. Bennett, *The Index of Leading Cultural Indicators*, 44–60.

2. Ibid, 46.
3. "Sex Among Teen Girls Increases," *The Dallas Morning News*, 5 January 1991.
4. "Census Reports a Sharp Increase Among Never-Married Mothers," *The New York Times*, 14 July 1993.
5. John Shelby Spong, *Living in Sin?: A Bishop Rethinks Human Sexuality* (San Francisco: Harper & Row, 1988), 52–53.
6. Leslie Wolfe, "And Baby Makes Two," *The Dallas Morning News*, 8 April 1992.
7. Ibid. Family's place in the social order goes beyond reproduction of the human species and instillation of values. The family likewise teaches the economic essentials: the "value of a dollar," the discipline of saving, and so on. The sober virtues of industry and thrift, so essential to the creation of lasting wealth, may come naturally to some. Still, these virtues need cultivation. The wealth that particular families may have accumulated devolves finally on the family's children—who are free to squander their inheritance, or, more constructively, to enlarge it. As George Gilder has noted, "After work the second principle of upward mobility is the maintenance of monogamous marriage and family . . . it is manifest that the maintenance of families is the key factor in reducing poverty" (*Wealth and Poverty* [New York: Basic Books, 1981], 69). Families likewise impart standards of health and cleanliness. These standards normally endure for a lifetime, to the point that old wives' tales— e.g., the danger of catching cold from going outside after a bath—are duly handed down as gospel.
8. Barbara Dafoe Whitehead, "Dan Quayle Was Right," *The Atlantic Monthly*, 271, 4, April 1993, 47–50, 52, 55, 58, 60–62, 64–66, 70–72, 74, 77, 80, 82, 84.
9. Ibid.
10. Carol Lawson, "When Baby Makes 2: More Women Choose Single Motherhood," *The New York Times*, 5 August 1993.

11. Ibid.
12. Anne Lamott, "Life Without Father Need Not Be Lonely," *The New York Times,* 5 August 1993.
13. Ibid.
14. Whitehead, "Dan Quayle Was Right."

Chapter 6

1. William Edward Hartpole Lecky, *History of European Morals from Augustus to Charlemagne,* vol. II (New York: D. Appleton and Company, 1908), 20–21.
2. Ibid.
3. At the time of *Roe v. Wade,* thirty states banned abortion entirely except to save the mother's life; two states and the District of Columbia banned it except to save the mother's life or health; Mississippi prohibited abortion except to save the mother's life or in cases of rape; thirteen states restricted abortion to cases involving rape, incest, a threat to the mother's life, or, in the baby's case, physical health damage or a grave physical defect. Four states by 1973 had repealed their abortion statutes; however, none permitted abortion after the fetus achieved viability (Source: Americans United for Life).
4. P. D. James, *The Children of Men* (New York: Knopf, 1993), 7–8.
5. "The Pope's Remarks to U.S. Bishops," *The New York Times,* 15 August 1993.
6. Richard Lamm, quoted in *Death/Dying,* ed. Bruno Leone (St. Paul: Greenhaven Press, 1986), 150.

Chapter 7

1. Jerome Kern/Oscar Hammerstein II, "All the Things You Are."
2. Tamar Lewin, "Canada Court Says Pornography Harms Women and Can Be Barred," *The New York Times,* 28 February 1993.
3. Ibid.

Chapter 8

1. Brinton, *A History of Western Morals*, 93.
2. Spong, *Living in Sin?*, 85.
3. Dean H. Hamer et al., "A Linkage Between DNA Markers on the X Chromosome and Male Sexual Orientation," *Science*, 261, 16 July 1993, 321–27.
4. Ibid.
5. Ruth Hubbard, "The Search for Sexual Identity," *The New York Times*, 2 August 1993.
6. "Gays Want Textbooks to Cite Homosexuality," *The Dallas Morning News*, 22 January 1992.
7. Felicity Barringer, "Sex Survey of American Men Finds 1% Are Gay," *The New York Times*, 15 April 1993.
8. Rita Kramer, *In Defense of the Family: Raising Children in America Today* (New York: Basic Books, 1983), 6.
9. "Beyond Rhetoric: A New American Agenda for Children and Families," Final Report of the National Commission on Children, 1991, xi.
10. Randy Shilts, *And the Band Played On: Politics, People, and the AIDS Epidemic* (New York: St. Martin's Press, 1987), 19.
11. "Beyond Rhetoric."
12. Irving Kristol, "AIDS and False Innocence," *The Wall Street Journal*, 6 August 1992.
13. Ibid.
14. *The New York Times*, 23 July 1993.

Chapter 9

1. Genesis 4:8.
2. Bennett, *Index of Leading Cultural Indicators*, 18–23.
3. Ibid., 4.
4. Ibid., 31.
5. "Parents, Leaders Hope to Stem Youth Violence," *The Dallas Morning News*, 9 September 1993.
6. Peter Kreeft, *Back to Virtue* (San Francisco: Ignatius Press, 1992), 25.
7. Genesis 9:6.
8. Deuteronomy 22:22.

9. "First, Reclaim the Streets," *The New York Times,* 1 January 1991.

10. Charles Murray, *Losing Ground: American Social Policy, 1950–1980* (New York: Basic Books, 1984).

Chapter 11

1. Robert L. Bartley, "'No Guardrails': Values Debate a Tectonic Clash," *The Wall Street Journal,* 14 April 1993.

2. Walter E. Williams, "A Dying Breed," Heritage Features Syndicate, 17 May 1989.

3. "Reality Check: Tom Wolfe Addresses the Real Estate Industry," *The Dallas Morning News,* 3 October 1993.

4. "A Catechism," *The Book of Common Prayer* (1928 version), various editions, 579–80.

Chapter 12

1. Alexis de Tocqueville, *Democracy in America,* vol. I, trans. Henry Reeve, (New Rochelle: Arlington House, 1965), 298, 296.

2. "Voices," *The Los Angeles Times,* 2 May 1992.

3. Ibid.

4. Psalm 8:5.

Chapter 13

1. "Polls Show Growth in Religious Belief," *The Christian Science Monitor,* 20 May 1993. Pollster George Gallup, Jr., himself says that only about 10 percent are wholly dedicated to their faith, religious commitment in America being far wider than it is deep. ("Religion in U.S. Termed a Lot of Show and Tell with Little Depth," *St. Petersburg Times,* 19 May 1990.)

2. Matthew 25:40.

3. Matthew 6:33.

4. Spong, *Living in Sin?,* 217.

5. "Church Writings on Sex May Spark Revolt from Pews," *The Washington Times,* 21 January 1992.

Chapter 14

1. T. Harry Williams, Richard N. Current, and Frank Freidel, *A History of the United States* (New York: Knopf, 1959), 402.

2. Russel Blaine Nye, *The Cultural Life of the New Nation* (New York: Harper and Bros. [The New American Nation Series], 1960), 43.

3. "Teen-Agers Called Shrewd Judges of Risk," *The New York Times*, 2 March 1993; Bennett, *Index of Leading Cultural Indicators*, 12; "Odds and Ends," *The Wall Street Journal*, 17 March 1993.

4. William J. Bennett, *The De-Valuing of America: The Fight for Our Culture and Our Children* (New York: Summit Books, 1992), 71.

5. William Celis, "School Choice Plan on Ballot in Colorado Puts State in Spotlight," *The New York Times*, 16 September 1992.

6. Laura Mansnerus, "Kids of the 90's: A Bolder Breed," *The New York Times*, "Special Report," 1993.

7. Ibid.

8. Ibid.

9. Thomas Sowell, *Inside American Education: The Decline, the Deception, the Dogmas* (New York: The Free Press), 35.

10. Ibid., 48.

11. Ibid., 49.

12. "Survey Shows U.S. Children Write Rarely and Not Well," *The New York Times*, 17 April 1992.

13. E. D. Hirsch, Jr., *Cultural Literacy: What Every American Needs to Know* (Boston: Houghton Mifflin, 1987), 2.

14. Thomas J. Fleming, "Egalitarianism, Centralization, and the Debasement of American Education," *Essays in Political Economy*, The Ludwig von Mises Institute, 9 July 1991.

Chapter 15

1. "What Are We Doing to the Young?" *Human Life Review*, 19, 4, Fall 1993, 93.

2. William Murchison, "The Straight '90s," *Human Life Review,* 19, 3, Summer 1993, 12.
3. *Safe Sex* (Grand Rapids: Baker Book House, 1992), 40–41.

Chapter 16
1. Shawn Sullivan, "Wife-Beating N the Hood," *The Wall Street Journal,* 6 July 1993.

Chapter 17
1. "God and the Ghetto," *The Wall Street Journal,* 25 February 1993.
2. Quoted in Russell Kirk, *The Conservative Mind: From Burke to Eliot,* 7th rev. ed. (Chicago; Washington: Regnery Books, 1986), 439.